BECOME THE BOSS MD

BECOME THE
BOSS MD

Success beyond
Residency

Amy Vertrees, MD

Creator and Host of the **BOSS: Business of Surgery Series** podcast

LIONCREST
PUBLISHING

BECOME THE BOSS MD
Success beyond Residency

FIRST EDITION

ISBN   978-1-5445-4295-9 *Hardcover*
         978-1-5445-4293-5 *Paperback*
         978-1-5445-4294-2 *Ebook*
         978-1-5445-4296-6 *Audiobook*

To my fellow BOSS MDs: You have always been the hero of your story.

CONTENTS

INTRODUCTION

Julia slumps into her car, pulls off her surgical mask and unclips her ID badge. For a moment she stares at her name, followed by those two small letters she's worked so hard to earn: MD.

Her own smiling face beams back. The photo was taken a week before Julia started this hospital job, her first as an attending general surgeon. It shows a hopeful young woman about to finally realize her dreams.

Julia exhales, tossing the badge aside. Her head still pounds from a tense staff meeting about declining reimbursements and more changes to the clinical structure. She needs to call hospital administrators about a confusing change to her contract. Then there's that pile of unfinished clinical notes. Her work day is over, but Julia's work will continue for hours at home (interrupted by intrusive thoughts about a recent gut-wrenching complication in the operating room).

Throughout medical school and residency, Julia logged countless demanding hours in lecture halls, labs, and clinics—running on ramen noodles, caffeine, and merciful energy reserves that always seemed to know when to kick in. Somehow, a concentrated mix of passion and adrenaline had kept her focused, driven, and moving toward the goal: becoming a physician—helping people, saving lives.

Now that she's finally arrived, where has all the energy gone?

YOU GOT THIS (REALLY!)

If you relate to the scene above, you're not alone. "Julia" may be fictional, but her story represents both my personal experience and anecdotes from physicians I've either supported through my professional coaching business or interviewed for my *Business of Surgery Series (BOSS)* podcast.

Despite ranking among the most educated professionals on the planet, we physicians too often find ourselves disempowered, overwhelmed, and utterly spent—not to mention, vastly underprepared to handle the business side of medicine.

From negotiating that first position to understanding billing and reimbursements to managing malpractice risks and dealing with difficult colleagues—our professional lives extend far beyond the clinical skills we're taught in residency. Over time, these daily challenges accumulate, eroding the joys of patient care.

Exhausted and disillusioned, we battle self-doubt, struggling to reclaim that sense of achievement we enjoyed during training. Some days it feels irreparably lost.

It's not.

It may not feel like it right now, but you've still got it. That energy and passion for your work—it's all still in there, and you can recover it. Not by doing less, but by doing things differently. Not by changing your job (necessarily), but by changing your perspective and approach.

The burnout narrative disempowers physicians. It reduces us to overworked, powerless victims of external forces. This keeps us looking outside, expecting someone else to solve our problems. We think administrators should find patients to grow our practice, or that insurance companies should magically transform overnight. Worn down by the money cycle complexities and administrative pressures, we rehearse stories of injustice and futility, further draining our energy and straining our business relationships.

It's time to challenge these stories and examine how you interact with the medical world. Your lifelong dream of becoming a doctor does not have to devolve into a recurring bureaucratic nightmare. In fact, your medical career can and should feel empowering and enriching—in spite of it all.

How do I know? Because I've been there: fed up with the never-ending demands of a flawed medical system, frustrated by my lack of influence and autonomy—until I began to make small but powerful changes in how I show up for myself and how I engage with my life's work.

MY BACKGROUND

I write this as someone very well-acquainted with both over-achievement and imposter syndrome. These interconnected (if seemingly opposed) forces of self-sabotage really blossomed in my teens.

Laser-focused on becoming a doctor, I was accepted into an early admission program allowing me to skip my senior year of high school and enroll at Georgia Tech—where I promptly became a member of the American Medical Students Association and president of the Georgia Tech pre-med society.

Still, by the end of undergrad, I'd somehow convinced myself I wasn't cut out for medicine. I resolved to earn my PhD in cell biology and anatomy. Before long, I began to doubt this move too. Although I learned how to be a better student and teacher, graduate school felt like a cop-out. I'd given into my insecurities, and I wasn't sure how to get back to my true path. After completing roughly master's level work, I left grad school without a degree and became an underwriter for home equity lines of credit.

Analyzing mortgage risks and liabilities may not have nourished my soul, but it provided a practical crash course in finance, exposing me to new concepts and professional interactions. Before long, though, medicine called me back.

I began teaching MCAT courses at Kaplan University and took a job as a medical assistant at an OB-GYN office. There, I learned how a medical office runs from the perspective of support staff.

In 2000, I hopped back on the high-achievement train, enrolling in medical school at the Uniformed Services University of the Health Sciences. There, I became an Army officer and graduated near the top of my class.

My general surgery residency took place at the Washington, DC Walter Reed Medical Army Center between 2004 and 2010—at the heights of both wars. I was deployed to three general surgery combat tours, one in Iraq and two in Afghanistan. Out in the field with sky-high stakes, seemingly impossible situations, and limited support, I had no choice but to become both self-reliant and resourceful—to trust my own leadership instincts and work effectively with those around me.

Between and after deployments, I served the American College of Surgeons (ACS) as president of the DC chapter's Young Surgeons Committee. To fill seats at meetings, I developed material that would lay the foundation of my *BOSS: Business of Surgery Series* podcast and coaching work. I figured if I needed to know these lessons, then others did, too.

Not that it boosted meeting attendance among residents. There's little urgency to learn new skills until practical challenges arise. Still, creating the ACS program helped me better understand the business and interpersonal aspects of medicine.

One key business lesson I've learned is when you're the tip of the spear, no one tells you you're on the right track. While I received good feedback from those who came, it was hard to stay motivated with low attendance, so the BOSS program took a five-year break.

Then came 2020, the COVID-19 pandemic, and the existential

and professional turbulence accompanying it. That year also brought the end of my contract at a regional health system. I didn't realize how unhappy I'd become until a coach asked me: "What are you tolerating?"

The truth I'd been hiding from myself was that I felt dissatisfied, disempowered, and stuck. After one particularly frustrating meeting, I spoke to the CEO to suggest ways to improve how we operated. On hearing that things would not change, I heard myself calmly respond, "Then I'm not interested in doing this anymore."

I wasn't miserable. This was, by most accounts, a good job. But after the self-reliance I'd gained in combat zones and the business acumen I'd developed through financial planning and ACS leadership—not to mention more than a decade of medical experience—I felt I should have more autonomy and influence. Sure, I could have renewed my contract, numbed myself into complacency, and tolerated another fifteen years of suppressed aggravation—but I just couldn't shake the feeling that *there had to be more than this.*

"Are you putting in your resignation notice?" I was asked.

"Yes," I replied suddenly—confidently. "I am."

While I hadn't planned to abruptly quit my job (and it understandably surprised my husband) this felt like a clear, conscious choice. As I walked out of the building, I envisioned myself clipping the tethers binding me to an old way of operating in the medical field—and felt a surge of energy and new possibilities.

WHAT YOU'LL LEARN

After nearly a decade of medical training, receiving that coveted white coat feels like you've finally *arrived*. Sure, you'll improve on your skills, adapt to new tech, pick up new tricks here and there—but, after residency, the hard learning's behind you, right?

Well, yes and no.

Residency taught you clinical skills. From here on out, you have many new skills to master—without the relative support and clear benchmarks of a linear training model. Unfortunately, most newly minted physicians have no idea these lessons are coming.

Luckily, you now have a guide to help. This book compiles lessons I've learned (and continue to learn) as a full-time surgeon, podcaster, and coach for other physicians. Consider this a starting point to lifelong learning—the guide you didn't know you needed.

If you've picked up this book as a more experienced physician, you may be experiencing self-doubts or mounting frustration as cost pressures, declining reimbursements, and high patient volumes have you rushing from room to room.

Or maybe you're just starting out as an attending, struggling to compete, self-promote, and fill your schedule. Meanwhile, tensions may be simmering—or even erupting—among equally burned out colleagues, administrators, and support staff.

Either way, you struggle to understand the ever-changing intricacies of malpractice risks, reimbursements, and insurance contracts—not to mention your own employment contract, which likely restricts how and where you can practice, should you choose to leave your job. Besides, with so much educational debt to pay down, why take risks or make waves?

The first thing to know is that feeling worn down by the gritty realities of our medical system doesn't make you a bad doctor. You are not an imposter, and you're not a failure. You're also not some helpless victim. You can, and should, stand up for yourself not just in the clinic, but with every contractual agreement you sign.

What you are, in fact, is a badass BOSS MD. You already have what it takes; you just have to find it. To help, this book offers fresh perspectives, a dash of supplementary information here and there—and many simple yet powerful mindset shifts.

We'll start in Part 1 with establishing your career, including examining your own strengths and how those match up to the career choices available to you (spoiler alert: you have more options than you think). This section also provides practical tips for nailing job interviews and negotiating contracts.

Part 2 will help you find your voice within the medical field. From marketing your practice to speaking up in difficult meetings to lobbying for causes, we'll explore self-advocacy and relationship management, both one-on-one and in groups.

Next, Part 3 focuses on improving outcomes. We'll unpack how to address and recover from complications, measure your own performance, take more efficient and effective clinical notes, and delegate without power struggles or undue effort.

Then it's time to "follow the money" with Part 4. This provides a primer on navigating coding and reimbursements, helping you get paid, avoid pitfalls, and better budget your clinical resources. (Don't worry; it's not as hard as you think.)

Finally, Part 5 deals with protecting your personal assets. We'll deconstruct the "never-enough" deficiency mindset, mitigate malpractice risks, cultivate abundance, and embrace career shifts.

While some of this content may sound technical, don't expect a dry, comprehensive encyclopedia of business concepts. Instead, this book offers an integrated eagle's eye view of the—real and perceived—hassles and hardships facing doctors in the US. We'll examine the bigger-picture systems at play—including how you fit into those, and what you can (and cannot) do about it all.

As medical students and residents, we develop a deep, sophisticated appreciation of interconnected anatomical and physiological systems. When applied to patient care, this informs how we ask questions and make connections to diagnose, treat, and problem-solve. It's time to apply that same approach to all aspects of your medical career.

Through it all, we'll focus mainly on how your mindset and habits—your limiting beliefs, thoughts, and patterns—determine how you progress within your career, care for your patients, and influence the medical field.

You'll find "Next Steps" at the end of each chapter to help you reflect and apply what you learn, plus suggested *BOSS* podcast episodes where you can find more information on certain topics.

YOUR HERO'S JOURNEY

The most compelling stories in books and films always involve conflict and frustration. Imagine, if you will: Our fearless protagonist sets out on a noble quest—to become a doctor, to help and heal. She faces detours, forks in the road, and obstacles galore. Then something happens to set off a chain of events which reset her course.

Granted, clinical notes and malpractice suits aren't exactly the stuff of literary or cinematic magic. In real life, resetting the course happens gradually. It often begins when mounting dissatisfaction leads physicians to start questioning everything.

It doesn't help that we enter the field with little to no practical training on the business aspects of medicine. Overwhelmed, we look for external solutions, but here's the thing: *We* are the ones who can best solve our problems. Stressors may build up over time, but our capacity to change also increases with experience and conscious effort. Our choices—big and small—serve as catalysts for our own plot twists.

When you own the story, you own the ending.

Stop looking outside yourself. This is *your* hero's journey. You are the one who determines your course. The first step is to get out of your own way. Once you clear your vision from personal and collective misconceptions, you can better see—and forge—your own path forward.

Let's begin by taking a hard look within. After all, more than anything else, the protagonist drives the story. If you want to become the hero of your own story, it's time for a thorough intake and examination—of yourself.

PART 1

ESTABLISH YOUR CAREER

CHAPTER 1

SELF EXAMINATION

It's not that Julia can't handle pressure. The high stakes, fast-paced precision of the operating room energizes her. The main issues lie outside the OR suite. Between all the paperwork, interpersonal tensions, and time pressures, Julia feels like some cog in a system she barely understands and feels powerless to control.

Where did it all go wrong? Julia wonders. She knows the nuts and bolts of surgery—and loves patient interactions. In fact, that's part of the problem. To maximize reimbursements, she's been asked to shorten patient visits. She's been compensating by giving patients her full attention—which means more incomplete notes to catch up on later.

Maybe this large hospital setting isn't for me, she thinks. Still, should she leave after barely one year? Then there's the stress of job hunting—weighing different options, poring over multiple applications, preparing for interviews.

Suddenly, she recalls an interaction with her program director. He'd asked her a simple question: *What are your strengths and weaknesses?*

Without thinking, she replied: "I'm an anxious person, but also a procrastinator."

As for strengths, Julia had to pause. Finally she said, "I'm a quick study and an excellent surgeon. I strive for perfection." Beyond that…Julia wasn't really sure.

GET HONEST

Any good story starts with a great character. As the hero of your story, you must get to know yourself. But to do that, you have to get all the way honest.

I've been out of residency since 2010, but only recently have I fully appreciated the value of fearless, candid self examination. Whether in the OR or in a meeting, the results of our actions and interactions depend primarily on us. Specifically: What we tell ourselves about both who we are and how others perceive us.

In other words, your thoughts really do create your reality.

This lesson lays the foundation for all you do. Your stories impact your habits, and your habits define your life. As we'll unpack more in later chapters: How you do one thing impacts how you do everything else—and it's all rooted in self-talk.

I struggled with stereotypes, causing me to interact in ways that didn't always serve me or those around me. To better compete (or so I thought), I leaned into the image of the domineering surgeon, barking orders—even making people cry.

In short, I was not a huge inspiration to residents and interns. In fact, I likely scared people away from surgery. Like Julia, I lacked agency, impact, and job satisfaction because I didn't know myself. I'd never questioned my stories or examined my unique strengths, goals, and needs.

This chapter will help you assess your own professional profile—then use that information to forge *your* version of success.

Remember: You're not being graded. This is for you—to help you both understand and *celebrate* yourself.

Drop self-judgment and lean in with self-compassion and curiosity. It's time to stop crapping on yourself, adjust your thought processes, and leverage your BOSS strengths.

KNOW THYSELF

Instead of chasing what you assume to be other people's expectations of you, take time to actually get to know yourself. You can gather this information in various ways, but the main questions include:

- What are my strengths?
- What are areas I could improve on?
- How do I interact with others?
- What do I actually want?

SELF-ASSESSMENT

Look back to times of conflict. When you're most compromised mentally and physically, which aspects of your job feel easiest? Which feel most taxing? Those tasks and responsibilities you gravitate toward "at your worst" can help you identify both your strengths and your professional values.

One fun, easy way to explore all these questions is through personality quizzes and questionnaires. Some free or inexpensive online self assessments I recommend include the Enneagram, Sparketypes, Clifton Strengths, and the "Stop Self-Sabotage" quiz.

These resources provide starting points for getting to know yourself, or at least which questions to ask. However, they're only as good as your own self-awareness.

We've all known people who claim certain traits, yet demonstrate the opposite. It's also true that we sometimes criticize others for the very things we don't want to admit about ourselves. Self-assessments are only as good as our own self-awareness. After all, they're informed by our—often limiting—thoughts about ourselves. If we're in denial about key aspects of our personalities or don't see how we're limiting ourselves, the results won't align with reality.

In short, crap in = crap out.

ASK FOR–AND BE WILLING TO RECEIVE–FEEDBACK

Ask other people—friends, mentors, family, colleagues, a therapist—to reflect on similar questions. What do they think you're good at? What might be some areas you could work on? How would they describe your interactions with others? What do they consider to be your core values?

Again, release self-judgment. Hold space for all information—especially when you don't like what you hear. It's all just feedback, something to keep in mind and change if needed. Nobody's perfect, and everyone brings something different to the table.

Remember that strengths and challenges—indeed your entire personality and patterns of moving through the world—will change and grow. We are not CT scan images frozen in time. We're more like surgeons, dissecting and removing what doesn't serve, modifying other parts to create better versions of ourselves.

SO, WHAT DO YOU WANT?

Many new physicians have trouble articulating the answer to this question—largely because they're out of practice.

In residency, goals are set for you. Once you break out of residency hustle culture, you dive headlong into another—one you've never been trained to manage.

It's time to set goals and make choices yourself: What kind of patients and cases do you want to accept? What hours do you want to work? Which practice model aligns with your personal preferences, needs, and values? This abrupt shift can feel liberating or paralyzing (or both at once).

Paradoxically, one of the best ways to figure out what you want is to identify what you *don't want*. Listen to what you complain about. If—like Julia—you gripe about rushed patient interactions in the large hospital setting, you might prefer the more relaxed atmosphere and family feel of private practice.

Your frenemies provide insight as well. Let's admit it; envy reveals desire. Who are the people you both admire and secretly can't stand? Get brutally honest with yourself about who you simultaneously respect and resent—and why. What roles do these people serve, and how do they operate within those?

Do you find yourself overly critical of people in leadership roles? Maybe you'd secretly like to run a practice of your own, but you don't know where to start.

Do you begrudge friends and family members with better work-life balance? Maybe you'd choose a more flexible career route if you didn't feel tied to the grind.

These feelings suggest qualities or lifestyles you wish you had, as well as stories you may be telling yourself. Let's dig deeper into those stories.

ASSESS THE ASSESSMENT

After gathering information about yourself—whether through quizzes, asking others, or examining self-talk—take a moment to jot down the results: What did your personality quizzes reveal? What did friends and associates say about you? What might your complaints and resentments reveal about your strengths and goals?

Next, question everything. How much of this is actually true? How much of it reflects limitations you put on yourself or perceived expectations of others?

If you're seeing trends in terms of what you and others see as your strengths, those likely represent professional and interpersonal superpowers you can leverage to everyone's advantage.

Then again, you may notice contradictions between what you assume about yourself and what others reported. This could reveal aspects of your personality you'd rather downplay or deny. You may consider your organizational skills and leadership qualities to be strengths—while others find you too rigid and uncompromising.

TRAITS VERSUS. CHOICES

If you uncovered prickly feedback like this, nice work! Now you have more data about past patterns to help inform your future choices.

Remember: How you show up for yourself and others is a verb, not a noun—a dynamic process, not a fixed identity. When confronted with negative feedback, don't panic. Take a beat and look for opportunities to grow or change.

The above example offers great insight into how true strengths—organization and decision making—can become weaknesses in the wrong context. In this case, mindfully choosing to listen more and practice more trust and collaboration could balance things out.

While we're all capable of over-inflating strengths, I find that—like Julia—most physicians are actually too hard on themselves. This happens when we over-identify with perceived flaws. Often, when I ask coaching clients about their weaknesses, they say something like Julia's comment: "I'm a procrastinator."

Revise the script. Instead of "I'm a procrastinator," try: "I'm a person who procrastinates."

Next, take it a step further: "I'm a person who in the past has procrastinated."

This reframes an apparently fixed personality flaw as an active, dynamic process. Thoughts and habits are not facts. They're choices that repeat until they become patterns. While patterns help predict the future, you can change the trajectory by shifting the dial—by choosing to more consistently show up in a slightly different way.

Byron Katie, considered by many to be the mother of modern coaching, developed a great method for evaluating our thoughts—the first step is reframing thoughts as choices.

It all comes down to four questions, which she calls "the work."

1. Is this thought true?
2. Can I absolutely know it's true?
3. How do I react—what happens—when I believe it's true?
4. Who would I be without this thought?

When you lean into the idea that you're a procrastinator, you're more likely to procrastinate. Meanwhile, you're ignoring all the times when you don't behave this way. Similarly, when you label yourself as an anxious person, you overlook times when you've shown up with confidence.

SELF-LIMITING BELIEFS

When faced with a negative thought, ask: *Where did this thought come from?*

Maybe it's something your dad or coach said when you were little, and you accepted it. Perhaps it's rooted in cultural stereotypes about how you should present yourself—like the overbearing, arrogant surgeon I once thought I had to be. Maybe you're selling yourself short because you're unnecessarily comparing yourself to others.

Your mind offers you thoughts all the time. You do not have to believe them. Once you start questioning those thoughts and beliefs, you can reframe or discard those that don't serve you.

In other words, you have much more control over who you are—and who you become—than you think.

FROM PROBLEM TO POTENTIAL

Julia would be surprised to hear that, although her anxiety creates issues, it's rooted in something positive, and it can be discarded or reframed as a strength. Sure, anxiety can be maladaptive—leading to avoidance patterns like procrastination—but at its root, Julia's anxiety means she deeply cares about the outcome. That's certainly not a bad thing.

Plus, she always gets it done—if under pressure, where she thrives best.

Resist the impulse to identify with perceived negative traits and reinforce the pattern ("I'm a procrastinator"). Instead shift your story from: "This is who I am," to: "This is how I've operated before—and I can change that."

It took me years to separate what I thought was expected of me from my true strengths. I didn't need to put on some hard-ass authoritative front to prove myself in the operating room. In fact, when I began showing up in a more authentic way, I got more respect, not less.

Ironically, my true strengths couldn't be farther from the persona I struggled to adopt early on. At my best, I'm a supportive mentor and coach, and an empathetic leader. Even when exhausted, I always find time and energy to give a pep talk to a colleague or comfort a patient. Understanding and leveraging strengths led me to find my best personal fit within the medical field—then launch a successful physician coaching program on the side.

DEFINE SUCCESS FOR YOU

It all begins with separating your so-called "identity" from patterns of thought and behavior that you can change. Your perceived "weaknesses" may just be actions and reactions that have not worked for you in the past. You can make better choices moving forward—choices that leverage your strengths and honor your personal and professional goals and values.

Now: *What does success look like to you?*

I started out my career with a vast, unhelpful collection of "shoulds." They followed me even into private practice: I *should* maintain a certain number of patients or cases at all times. I *should* make myself available for everyone at all times. Others *should* show respect for me in strictly defined ways. I assumed all of this would be harder because I'm a woman.

These assumptions disempowered both me and those around me. Why? Because they were rooted in what I considered to be the expectations of other people. None of them leveraged— or even considered—either my superpowers or my personal definition of success.

Just like our goals and personality traits, our definition of success changes over time. During med school and residency, "success" comes prepackaged. Once you leave that training model, it's time to ditch the "shoulds" and figure it out for yourself: What do *you* want—and why? Where do you want to go—and how can you get there?

Otherwise, you may also find yourself asking, "Where did it all go wrong?" Like Julia, we may not realize we've been chasing externally imposed goals until we graduate and have to come up with new ones.

Once you understand better what you want and what you bring to the table, assess your professional options. In Chapter 2 we'll talk about finding a path that aligns with your goals, strengths, and values—and realizes your personal vision of success.

NEXT STEPS

1. Take the personal assessments below to explore what you think of yourself right now.
2. Ask two or three people who know you well to name your three top strengths, plus one area you can work on.
3. Examine the picture that emerges. Does this sound like you? Can you lead more with your strengths? What areas do you want to develop?
4. Challenge beliefs keeping you from becoming the person you want to be.

RESOURCES:

Clifton Strengths: https://www.gallup.com/cliftonstrengths/en/254033/strengthsfinder.aspx

Enneagram: https://www.enneagraminstitute.com/rheti

Sparketypes: https://sparketype.com/

Stop Self-Sabotage: https://www.drjudyho.com/stopselfsabotagequiz

CHAPTER 2

CAREER OPTIONS

Julia's alarm pierces her sleep, pulling her into the usual morning clockwork: shower, fresh scrubs, coffee, clip on the ID badge, and hit the road. She spends this commute—and most of the morning clinic—fretting about a meeting with the head of the department.

He wanted to discuss vague "changes" to her schedule. She walks to the meeting room like she's been called into the principal's office, racking her brain for potential blunders—incomplete paperwork, dissatisfied patients, anything.

It starts off well: "You're doing a good job. We hear great things," he says, "but—your numbers are still too low, and it's going to affect your compensation, not to mention your productivity bonus. So we've added an afternoon clinic for you. You'll also have to shorten your patient visits again. Keep them under fifteen minutes each."

After a pause, Julia asks, "Do I have any say over how this gets arranged?"

"No, no, the schedule is set. Also, a patient complained about you last week, so be mindful that those patient satisfaction scores also impact your bonus moving forward."

Julia leaves the meeting deflated. All she ever wanted to do was become a doctor, not to fret about numbers all day. Now she feels trapped in a machine based on convoluted and constantly changing metrics determining how she gets paid, with little to no time for the relationship building she loves.

No wonder a patient complained, she thinks. *I don't like who I am becoming, either. Maybe it's time to look at other options.*

THE FULL LANDSCAPE

Like Julia, many physicians are naturally responsible rule-followers who thrived within the clear parameters of medical training. I'm certainly one. Residency immerses us in an academic clinical setting, so most of us automatically look for the next pre-established formula or track to follow into the rest of our medical careers.

In other words, instead of considering all our options, we look for the path we're "supposed to take." This often leads us to work in large hospitals or medical systems without examining whether those environments best suit us.

The first step, of course (per Chapter 1) is taking the time to better get to know who you are, how you operate, and what you want. If Julia had been encouraged to do the same, she may have recognized earlier that her passion lies not only in the operating room, but also in developing meaningful patient relationships. Then, she might have selected a career path that leads closer to that goal.

This chapter zooms out to survey the broader landscape of professional options available to physicians. With better self-knowledge and a fuller understanding of the industry, you can pick the right direction for your hero's journey and become your own unique version of the BOSS MD.

TAKE YOUR TIME

Residency training mainly takes place within the academic medical program approved by ACGME (Accreditation Council for Graduate Medical Education), which standardizes rotations to meet evolving training metrics. While this model is great for yielding specific, predictable results for board certification, it does not reflect all practice options.

If you choose the wrong opportunity and decide to change course, that doesn't mean you've failed—and you're certainly not alone. According to a 2019 nationwide survey published in the peer-reviewed journal *Surgery*, the roughly three-year attrition rate for first surgery jobs is at least 44 percent. It's perfectly normal to move around until you find the right fit—and to outgrow a previously good fit and move on. Every experience teaches you something worthwhile, if you know how to look for it.

That said, job hopping has its costs. Each time you move from one salaried position to another, you incur expenses, lose patients, and rebuild from scratch. Plus, you must insure yourself against potential malpractice suits between jobs, and you may be restricted by your previous contract in terms of where and how you can practice.

When selecting a first job or considering a professional move—check your expectations. There's no such thing as a "perfect" job and no career shift will solve all your problems. As discussed in Chapter 1, if you're committed to negative stories and patterns, you will bring those along wherever you go.

Still, you'll thrive best where you can lead with your strengths, goals, and values. So take your time and explore all options. There are several kinds of work available to physicians, including:

- The employed model, typically in a hospital or medical system
- Private practice, as a partner or solo practitioner (often in association with a practice management company)
- Academic medicine, which includes teaching and research
- Locum tenens, as an independent contractor
- Non-clinical options—which may involve additional training—such as medical consulting, healthcare administration, or working for a medical device company

PROTECT YOUR NPI

If you want to practice medicine in almost any capacity, you will need an active National Provider Identifier (NPI) number. The Centers for Medicare and Medicaid issue this unique, ten-digit number to every physician accepting Medicare or Medicaid. Commercial healthcare insurers and other payers have since adopted use of the NPI for prescription and billing purposes.

Think of the NPI like a social security number for health care providers. Use it sparingly and protect it. Much like your SSN, an NPI can be "stolen" and submitted along with fraudulent Medicare and Medicaid claims for reimbursement.

Compared to your SSN, it's harder to keep the NPI private, but you can monitor your claims and reimbursements to make sure they match your actual clinical activities and records—just as you regularly check your credit report.

LOCATION, LOCATION, LOCATION

Before we launch into those practice models and non-clinical options, let's take a moment to consider, in the most literal terms, *where* you want to be.

What you do at work constitutes one part of your life. You also need to find the setting and community that supports your lifestyle, ideal home life, and career goals. If you're not somewhere that fulfills both your professional and personal needs, you're not likely to thrive, regardless of the job.

First, consider what you value in a home base. Would you rather be close to family or connected to cultural events? Are you planning to have children? If so, you'll want to think about school districts and maybe family support.

Next, think about the size, character, and career implications of your ideal community. If you're a big city person, you may crave opportunities to socialize or pursue interests. Just keep in mind the implications for your chosen specialty. Within large urban settings, you'll likely face more competition than in smaller metropolitan areas. This oversaturated supply combined with a higher cost of living may result in lower pay.

If you're, say, a hepatobiliary surgeon, your opportunities to practice within your hyper-specialized field of expertise may be limited to larger communities. But if you don't love city life, you'll need to either adjust to a long commute or be willing to mainly take general call. Meanwhile, if you prefer a broad general practice but wish to live in downtown Manhattan, you'll have to compete with all the New York City specialists.

In more rural areas, you'll face less competition, but also less support for specialized problems—not to mention more cultural and professional isolation. But if you're a general practice physician who loves the great outdoors and a broad practice, that may be just the place for you.

EMPLOYED VERSUS PRIVATE MODELS

In 2021, the American Medical Association (AMA) reported that most physicians work in larger hospitals and medical systems, rather than private practice. Market pressures associated with the COVID-19 pandemic exacerbated trends of practice acquisition and consolidation by hospitals and other corporate-owned medical systems.

Within a larger employed system, you may have more rules, which can get tedious or confusing. Plus, you might still have to operate under an eat-what-you-kill model that requires you to recruit your own patients and manage billing and reimbursement largely on your own.

In private practice, of course, you still have all of that to worry about. Even more so, in fact. If you run your own show, things like marketing and reimbursements not only determine how *you* get paid, but also how you pay everyone and everything else.

People often choose the employed setting in a misguided attempt to avoid these business aspects of medicine—only to discover they have to know and do this stuff anyway. Plus, they have less direct influence over how everything's managed.

It is possible to join a private practice—or even start your own—right out of residency. Some hospitals offer an income guarantee agreement, which acts as a forgivable loan for your first year's salary, provided you stick around for a certain period of time. When joining a private practice, you'll likely start out with a guaranteed salary—with or without an income guarantee agreement—for the first year or two as you build a patient following. If you aren't offered a base salary, you can at least negotiate a guaranteed draw for the first few months as you're getting started, even if you have to true-up later. The same goes for smaller non-profit hospitals and even some larger corporate-owned systems.

The bottom line is that, with both employed and private practice, you must have some awareness of business principles—marketing, coding, billing and reimbursement, insurance and malpractice compliance, etc.—to varying degrees.

ACADEMIC MEDICINE

Although most doctors move out of the academic model, we all start out there as residents. This environment provides exposure to and experience within different specialties and settings, helping us find our strengths and passions.

While academic medicine comprises a mix of private and employed models, the majority of academic physicians are employed by a university or teaching hospital. But compared to other employed models, they typically deal with less of the business end.

Good thing, too, since they need time to teach, assess student learning, develop curriculum, and conduct research. If you're a natural educator or scholar, this may be just the life for you.

Don't expect to be well compensated for these additional responsibilities. Academic physicians may enjoy less time worrying about business-related matters like recruiting patients, but they're typically paid less, despite potentially working more—often in a more urban place with a higher cost of living.

For many, the opportunity to research topics or educate students and residents offers its own reward. Plus, with academic medicine, you'll practice within cutting edge facilities using all the newest technologies and methods.

Let's be honest; you may face additional unpaid work regardless of which model of full-time practice you choose—whether administrative or academic in nature. So let's think back to your self-assessment of personal strengths and values. The question is: What brand of extra work do you find easier or more meaningful, interesting, and energizing?

LOCUM TENENS

Locum tenens offers the most flexible way to practice within any medical specialty. Rather than having one fixed job at one fixed location, you serve as a traveling independent contractor filling in as needed, particularly for physicians on extended sick leave, parental leave, or even private practice owners planning a long trip. In fact, the Latin term *locum tenens* roughly translates to "place holder" in English. Think of it as the medical equivalent of substitute teaching.

It used to be that locums jobs were considered second rate. The stereotype of "Larry Locums" was the guy who'd tried and failed to secure a salaried clinical position. Locums was seen as a backup plan if that first job didn't come through right away, or in the event that you lost a "good" job.

That perspective is changing. These days, people increasingly value locum tenens as a valid or even preferable alternative to the rigid restrictions of traditional employed and private models. Turns out, ultimate flexibility is worth a lot, too.

Plus, locum tenens pays well. After all, it must offset the loss of secured benefits (including malpractice, which contractors are required by law to have), and it allows you to travel, experience different practice settings, and easily adjust hours in response to having children, caring for an aging parent, or other life shifts.

Because locum tenens physicians aren't typically beholden to traditional non-compete clauses, if they never want to work at a certain hospital again, they may not have to move. They can work at the hospital across the street. However, if you start out as an employed physician, your contract may prohibit you from shifting even to locum tenens in that area.

For locums work, you still need to know your stuff when it comes to business: incorporating and maintaining your professional association (PA) or professional limited liability company (PLLC) status, marketing yourself, managing contracts, planning for taxes, finding the best malpractice policy, and tracking all business expenses and earnings.

NON CLINICAL

An increasing number of MDs and DOs are finding alternatives to clinical work. This goes to show that, despite those years of training, you're not tied to one particular professional track.

Some opt for an administrative role, such as chief medical officer. Often advanced degrees—like a master's of health administration (MHA) or an MBA in healthcare management— are required, or at least preferred, for something like this. At the very least, you'll need a good deal of medical experience and a proven aptitude for finance.

You can also find opportunities as a medical consultant. On my *BOSS* podcast, I spoke to a woman who got her MBA during residency, then split her professional life with a part-time role in academic endocrine surgery and part-time consulting on medical devices for a robotics company.

Regardless of what you do with your medical degree, understand that you have options—and it's okay to change course. Your career can and should evolve and grow with you.

Returning to our protagonist, Julia, it's possible she picked the wrong job right off the bat. For her, the large, for-profit hospital environment felt like a machine, perhaps because she never fully understood the full range of possibilities at her disposal. As Dr. Steve Siegal shared on an episode of the *BOSS* podcast, large hospital systems don't always understand what we're trained to do or how we can help them.

By the same token (as we'll explore in subsequent sections), maybe Julia simply never learned to acquire the right tools to thrive within her current environment.

Either way, information is key—about your own strengths and goals and which professional options best align with those. First, clarify where you want to go, then figure out how to get there.

This means competing within the right market, starting with how you show up for job interviews. Most professional candidates (in medicine and all fields) tend to approach interviews in a very limited and disempowering way—especially early in their careers. The next chapter reframes the job interview to help you gather the right information and maximize your negotiating power so you can make the best impression and the best choice.

NEXT STEPS

1. List career path options. What appeals to you about each? What are your deal breakers?
2. Explore what you want from a home base (cost of living, proximity to family)? What do you wish to avoid (traffic, snow)? How might location impact career options for your field?

3. Reach out to mentors and colleagues who practice in less traditional ways. Ask what they like and don't like about their work.

BUSINESS OF SURGERY SERIES (BOSS) PODCAST EPISODES:

https://www.BOSSsurgery.com/podcasts/
boss-business-of-surgery-series

Ep. 7: *Gaining Control of Your Career as a Locums Surgeon,* with Susan Trocciola

Ep. 17: *Pitfalls of Different Surgery Practice Models,* with Dr. Matt Endara

Ep. 22: *Lessons Everyone Should Hear on CVs,* with Dr. Emily Steinhagen

Ep. 66: *Location-Based Job Search,* with Dr. Amy Saleh

Ep. 58: *Finding the Right Practice,* with the Medical Matchmaker, Dr. Lara Hochman

Ep. 56: *Creating the Life You Want as a Community Surgery,* with Dr. Kathy Ma

---

CHAPTER 3

JOB INTERVIEWS

It took some research—including carefully mapping out which options lay outside the geography of her non-compete clause—but Julia found a couple of open surgery positions not too far away, including a smaller non-profit hospital and a private practice.

She's excited about new opportunities, but increasingly nervous about interviews. She spends hours online searching common questions and drafting and redrafting responses.

During the first interview, she finds herself over-explaining and laughing too much, trying to appear agreeable and give the "right" answers. On her drive home, she realizes she was so worried about not looking needy or greedy that she forgot to ask key questions about scheduling and compensation. Suddenly, new questions pop into her head, particularly in response to something the interviewer said.

"We're so happy you're here," he'd told her. "We've had so much turnover lately."

I wonder why, she thinks.

SHIFT YOUR MINDSET

Now that you know what you're looking for, it's time to nail those job interviews and discern which opportunity is right for you.

Most of us prepare for job interviews in a very disempowering way. We try to compete with other candidates—anticipating questions the interviewer might ask and answers they might want to hear. We behave like struggling actors auditioning for a big part, doing our best impressions of what we think the casting director wants.

Drop the act. As a BOSS MD, you don't need someone to cast you in the big show. No matter what happens, you are already the protagonist of your own story. Instead of proving yourself, focus on figuring out which job and career track best aligns with your unique strengths and values.

Think of each interview as mutual exploration between equals. You should interview them just as much as they're interviewing you. The conversation should never feel like one side pitted against the other, quietly evaluating while holding all the power. Instead, it should feel like a reciprocal exchange between grown adults with overlapping interests.

As a highly-trained professional with needs and goals of your own, come with your own questions. What are you looking for in terms of professional culture, workflow, and advancement?

Both this chapter and the next will help you figure out what questions to ask when job hunting and how to negotiate—even after they send a contract to sign. But first, take a moment to breathe, relax, and refocus.

CALM YOUR NERVES

Before an interview, dial down that fight-or-flight response. If on some level, you feel your survival and livelihood at stake, your autonomic nervous system will act accordingly, triggering fear, defensiveness, or mental paralysis.

It's normal to feel nervous about interviews, and you're not going to soothe your system by trying to deny or suppress nerves. Instead, accept anxiety as a natural response and decide in advance what to do about it. While you can't just turn off your autonomic stress response—poof!—you can find ways to shift that anxious energy into excitement and curiosity.

You can also tone it down through good, old-fashioned visualization, like imagining your interviewer in their underwear. It may seem cliche, but this classic technique really can help calm jitters and ground you in the moment. If that's too crude for your tastes, try imagining the interviewer as a child or inexperienced youth. Or think of someone you inherently trust and respect, then mentally connect the interviewer with that person. It helps to role play with someone safe and familiar. At the end of the day, all people are just people—including this stranger interviewing you.

Recognize how you behave under pressure. Maybe, like Julia, you ramble or laugh too loud. Remember, you're not there to perform. Just like the interviewer, you're there to gather information and evaluate professional fit. If you're not listening or showing up in an authentic way, how will you know if the opportunity fits *you*?

Take the spotlight off yourself. If a question catches you off guard, pause. It helps to buy time by asking a neutral question like, "I may not understand, can you repeat that?" Or, "Could you say more about what you mean by that?"

Getting nervous can feel like some huge weakness, but it doesn't have to be—if you meet it head on. No one expects you to be some stoic, emotionless robot. You can feel your feelings while adeptly navigating these conversations safely.

INFORMATION GATHERING

Before, during, and after the interview, the name of the game is info-gathering. I find social networks are the best places to get insights and honest reviews of medical practices by employed physicians, but take each workplace review with a grain of salt; everybody's having a subjective human experience. During the interview, you can ask to speak to physicians who currently work there or previously worked there. The worst they can say is no.

Start with open-ended questions like, "Could you describe the culture of this hospital?" Or "Please walk me through how your practice is run." How the recipient frames their response will tell you a lot about their professional priorities and values.

Potential employers want to know you've done basic homework on the community and patient base. If they ask why you've chosen their hospital or clinic as a place to work, avoid dismissive answers live, "I drive by here often—and after all, you offered me an interview." They want someone with genuine interest in rooting at their practice, becoming a member of the team, and providing value to their patients.

Follow up with more specific questions based on what you learn. If you started with workplace culture, ask for specific examples of their core values and whether those factor into employee performance reviews or bonuses.

Inquire about the current strengths and weaknesses of the practice, as well as their goals and strategies for the future. What are some challenges they're facing? Has there been significant turnover? What's their growth plan?

From there, get into the nuts and bolts of expectations and responsibilities, as well as clinical and call schedule expectations, compensation and more. As we'll explore in the next chapter, there are many common contract details you'll want to proactively discuss to secure both professional development opportunities and an exit strategy—before you sign the dotted line.

However—especially if you are coming straight from residency—that first job interview may not be the time or place to hit hard with negotiations. First, set the right tone. Your engagement, interest, and informed questions can all demonstrate that hiring you is an excellent choice.

TACTICAL EMPATHY

If the interviewer mentions a clear red flag, like high physician turnover, what's a tactful way to gather more information?

Don't lose sight of the fact that the interviewer is a human who—just like you—wants this interview to go well. As mentioned earlier, you can proceed in a way that puts everyone at ease. Employ some curiosity and what FBI negotiator Chris Voss (author of *Never Split the Difference*) calls "tactical empathy."

"You mentioned high turnover," you might say. Then, imagine how they must feel and express understanding: "That must be frustrating. What's your perception of what's happening?"

It's often helpful to leave delicate questions like this one open ended. If they cannot produce a clear answer, that's an answer in itself. You can also ask solution based follow ups like, "What steps are you taking not just to replace but to also retain people moving forward?"

The tone and attitude of the interviewer when speaking about challenges may reveal more red flags. If they seem paternalistic or dismissive, pay attention. Also note when you ask specific questions and they get avoidant, dodging pertinent details related to the contract, terms of pay, or other important issues that will directly impact your life.

FOCUS ON COLLABORATION

As a high achiever, you want to succeed in everything you do—but the truth is some opportunities aren't meant for you. Before you go into each job interview, first make it okay for this to not be a position you want, or one that wants you.

Each interview experience adds value, but you only need one job. If it turns out to not be the right fit, that doesn't mean you've failed. In fact, you've succeeded—at finding where you don't fit, which you want to figure out as soon as possible.

Remember that interviews and contract negotiations are not about you getting everything you want. They're about exploring the viability of and setting the groundwork for a mutually beneficial, potentially long-term relationship.

Earlier, I referenced FBI negotiator Chris Voss, author of *Never Split the Difference*. In that book, he talks about the importance of working towards collaboration during high stakes discussions. In addition to the concept of tactical empathy—which emphasizes understanding other experiences and perspectives—he discusses the benefit of taking a pause, as well as concepts like accusation audits and mirroring.

The accusation audit is a fancy term for proactively addressing fears about how you may come across. For example: "It may seem like I'm asking a lot of questions. I just want to make sure we have a good fit." By preemptively labeling a potential emotion or concern, you can neutralize misunderstanding or judgment.

Mirroring is simply repeating the last thing the interviewer said in the form of a question, such as: "Take call seven times a month?" Especially when used with a pause, this helps you buy time while you consider your response. Mirroring demonstrates not only that you understand, but also that something got your attention. You may find that the interviewer begins to clarify or expound in response to your neutral repetition of their comment. They may even backpedal to soften their position around something they now perceive as a potential problem for you.

Techniques like these help you stay grounded and empathetic during interviews, meetings, or any difficult conversations. I've used them at home. Recently, I let my daughter know she needed to clean out her closet—which she was not happy about, so I helped her start. Despite my ban on food upstairs, we found fossilized cookie dough in a bowl. To avoid knee-jerk defensiveness devolving into an argument, I said, "I'm not mad. You're not mad. Look, we're not mad. But it's my job as a parent to make sure you know how to follow rules."

A job interview is not an audition, and it's not a test. It's also not some one-and-done task. Forget about the competition and focus on getting acquainted and building a relationship.

When you go into a job interview thinking you *need this job* or that it will solve all your problems, you may have blinders on. Rather than accurately assessing the conversation, you'll write a fantasy about it.

Likewise, don't sell a fantasy about yourself. You don't want a job acquired under false pretenses; you want a true long-term fit. The only way to find that is by being yourself.

Be sure to lead with your personal strengths, advocate for your goals and values, and be discerning. Above all, stay curious and investigative—that's why you're in the interview. Otherwise—like Julia did in her first interview, you may miss details, potential red flags, or opportunities to set yourself up for success. You're there to investigate—not to prove your worth or knowledge—so don't assume you already know all the answers.

Of course, be sure to discuss this opportunity with your family.

The last thing you want to do is throw your heart and soul into an interview, get the job, and end up moving after two years because your partner or kids hate the area.

Even if an interview goes less than perfectly, there may still be time to negotiate. The next chapter will discuss details to keep in mind when reviewing a new contract—and how to negotiate key aspects of your contract before signing.

NEXT STEPS

1. How can you bring more of yourself to interviews? What impression do you want potential employers/colleagues to take away?
2. When exploring each job option—both before and after interviewing—list potential red flags associated with each opportunity.
3. During interviews (or any important conversation), practice strategies for collaboration and info-gathering: accusation audit, mirroring, tactical empathy, pauses.
4. Make sure people close to you are happy with your job choice. Ask for their input—before it becomes an expensive lesson.

BOSS PODCAST EPISODES:

https://www.BOSSsurgery.com/podcasts/
boss-business-of-surgery-series

Ep. 24: *Perspectives from a Surgery Program Director, with Dr. Jonathan Dort*

Ep. 40: *Surgery Training and Practice Are More Flexible than You Think, with Dr. Feibi Zheng*

Ep. 32: *Navigating an Important Meeting Replay*

CHAPTER 4

THE CONTRACT

When interviews left her with more questions than answers, Julia reached out to a friend who had recently signed a new contract. Over coffee, they chatted about job hunting pitfalls, including something Julia hadn't given much thought to.

"Do *not* slouch on the contract review!" he warned. "Read every word, and negotiate what doesn't sound right."

Julia had always assumed contracts, with their fine print and legal jargon, were set in stone—that negotiations ended with interviews. *Maybe it's not too late after all*, she now thinks.

This insight could not have come at a better time. Julia soon receives offers from both practices: a smaller hospital and a private practice.

Opening the contract from the "high turnover" hospital, she almost immediately notices something fishy. "Call schedule is arranged at the sole discretion of the employer," she reads and raises an eyebrow. From experience, Julia knows how quickly an unpredictable call schedule can consume her life.

Plus, she sees zero mention of the verbal promises the interviewer made about CME bonuses. Meanwhile, the non-compete clause is not just restricted to a certain mile radius around the practice location she'd be working at; it also includes areas around every location of the practice! And it appears that the hospital can terminate her for all kinds of vague reasons.

EVERYTHING IS NEGOTIABLE

Think of the interview as the setup and the contract as the close. In other words, if you haven't yet signed that dotted line, you can still negotiate.

It's common to hear things like, "This is our standard contract," or "This really isn't negotiable." But trust me—based on countless conversations with healthcare attorneys—it's all negotiable, depending on your leverage.

Ideally, the first step is to secure multiple offers—if at all possible. This provides leverage for you to increase your negotiating power. You'll be surprised by how much you can negotiate if you lead with confidence and trust—and you're sincerely willing to walk away.

Next, make sure you always *very carefully* read every line of your proposed contract. Note anything that seems unclear, contradictory, or potentially problematic. Don't be afraid to reach out and set up a follow up meeting to clarify terms of the contract.

Consult with legal counsel. Working with a lawyer shouldn't be scary or formal. Remember, your attorney is *your* advocate. They're able to walk you through the agreement, translating complicated terms and helping you determine which areas to negotiate.

Especially early in your career, you may worry that trying to negotiate terms of a job may brand you as needy or problematic, and they'll decide to go with someone else. Maybe they will. If so, *that's okay*. In fact, you probably dodged a bullet. A good employer wants to work with you to build a mutually beneficial relationship, not to hire the most submissive candidate.

The key to negotiating employment contracts is to emphasize the positive and identify issues to clarify and negotiate without coming across as hostile. You might say, "I'm very excited about this opportunity. I'm including a few key changes that, after discussing with my attorney, I'd like to edit in the current agreement. I'm happy to discuss at your convenience."

In other words, if an organization is worth working for, they fully expect you to take your time, ask questions, and advocate for yourself. You'll come across as someone who's well informed and knows what you want.

Solid negotiating sets you up not only for better terms or starting pay, but also for a steeper growth curve. If they see confidence and discernment, they may look to you for advancement possibilities down the road. While you can always adjust your trajectory later by requesting a raise or promotion, your strongest negotiating position is always before you sign.

Avoid falling into the trap of "we'll re-negotiate that later or include that as an amendment." The golden hour is not just for trauma; it also applies to that critical period before accepting a job. You may not get another chance to adjust terms once you've lost your pre-signing leverage.

THINGS TO LOOK FOR

Your contract should set the groundwork for a mutually beneficial long-term understanding between you and your employer. If the contract contradicts or neglects to mention verbal agreements, ask for those to be changed or added to the contract. Address anything that doesn't seem to align with your best interests, and consider hiring a healthcare attorney to provide evidence of something not being standard and increase your credibility during negotiations.

EXIT STRATEGY

It's critical to devise a fair exit strategy. Before you even walk in the door of a hospital or medical practice, secure your way out. Your contract may include non-compete clauses and other potential back-end pitfalls to look out for.

For the *BOSS* podcast, I spoke to Amanda Hill, JD, a healthcare attorney who advocates for physicians every day. Her suggestion was to "role play" the exit in your mind.

What might happen if you left? How much advance notice is required? How might this impact your income? You may want to wait a period of time before putting in your notice to make sure you get your bonus check (or avoid having to pay it back).

Review the non-compete range, and try to keep it as tight and close to where you work as possible. By thinking through everything involved in a potential exit, you'll be better equipped to negotiate on the front end.

Non Compete

Right now—during interviews and contract negotiations—you aren't exactly planning to leave. That's exactly why it's such a good time to figure out the details of a potential exit. In some ways, it's like a prenuptial agreement. The best time to review expectations and contingencies for a split is when both parties are in their right minds and getting along.

What happens if you move on from this position? Can you continue to practice in the area, or would you have to move?

In early 2023, the United States Federal Trade Commission announced the intention to broadly prohibit non-competition agreements—including within the medical field. But as I write this, the majority of hospitals and private practices still use them—and they vary widely from practice to practice, subject to different state laws and regulations.

Non-compete agreements can be a hot-button issue, but it's worth at least trying to negotiate more favorable terms. You might hear that a state will not enforce a non-compete clause, but banking on that is a gamble. Even if you don't think your non-compete is enforceable, it can spook and discourage potential employers.

Malpractice Nose and Tail Coverage

You may have heard about malpractice nose and tail coverage. These cover the same period of time: when you're no longer employed by a practice, but you're still within the statute of limitations for any potential lawsuit related to care you provided while there.

A tail policy is typically associated with a "claims made" professional malpractice policy, as opposed to the kind of "occurrence based" policy that doesn't require a tail. Make sure you know what type you have.

Typically, physicians can be sued for malpractice for up to two years after providing the care in question, sometimes more. The time period depends on both the law in your state and when an injury is considered "discovered." Let's say you're a surgeon who does an operation at Practice A. A few weeks later, you accept a new job with Practice B. Then, a month into your new job, you get sued for that operation you performed in Practice A. If your malpractice policy for Practice A lacked tail insurance, you won't be covered at all for this suit.

If you know the employer you're leaving won't cover your tail, it's absolutely vital to either negotiate nose coverage from your new job, or get a quote for an individual tail policy and see if your future employer will cover part or all of the cost. Nose coverage retroactively insures the time represented by the statute of limitations from a previous job—*before* you signed the new contract. But if you fail to secure this nose coverage, or you wait to negotiate one with your new employer until after a claim has been filed, you could end up paying for individual tail coverage yourself—to the tune of tens of thousands.

Termination Clauses

Termination clauses clarify who's allowed to cancel the contract and on what grounds. Most contracts specify termination without cause, which means that your three year contract may not be three years.

Make sure the termination clause allows you to unilaterally leave. Most of the time, there's a notice period—often around ninety days. Try to bake this into your contract both ways. A reasonable notice period ensures you'll have time to interview and secure a new contract while you still have a paycheck.

Also, pay attention to termination for cause sections with vague, ambiguous terms. Do you really want to be terminated immediately for cause because you "failed to follow company policy?" Were you first given notice of such failure with an opportunity to repair the situation?

GET IT IN WRITING

Like Julia, I wasn't aware of the "entire agreement clause" until recently, when I interviewed two attorneys for an episode of the *BOSS* podcast.

As one of them, Michael Johnson, Jr, Esq., explained, the clause basically stipulates that the terms of contract (the "entire agreement") can supersede and overrule any other agreements. Always remember that oral agreements, handshakes, and emails aren't considered legally binding.

This clause is often used to discredit or disregard oral agreements, including those made during interviews. In short, if it's not in writing *in that contract*, it's not enforceable by legal means. Just because they said it, doesn't mean they have to do it. Get what you want in writing—every time.

SUNSET CLAUSE

If you can't agree on a topic or something ends up missing from the contract and you identify it later, there might still be an option to rectify it via contract amendment—for example, by adding a sunset clause. This applies to rights or obligations that expire over a period of time. If you are offered a guaranteed salary as a loan, or asked for a personal guarantee, asking if it can be forgiven over time as you stay in the area may be a great way to minimize your financial risk.

VALUE BEYOND SALARY

When it comes to compensation and overall value, look at more than just your salary. If you have to relocate, negotiate moving expenses into your contract. You should also discuss additional compensation, including a sign-on bonus and continuing medical education (CME) reimbursements and bonuses, which both incentivize training and help offset dues and membership fees for professional organizations, tuition costs, book fees, and coaching.

In addition to finances, consider the value of your time, energy, flexibility, and lifestyle. Does the practice allow moonlighting? Do they offer adequate paid time off for sick leave, vacation, and bereavement? What about parental leave?

Make sure you carefully review the clinical schedule and the call schedule. These elements, which profoundly impact your work-life balance, can turn out to be just as important as your salary, if not more so. At the very least, make sure it's rotated fairly among all doctors.

As we saw in Julia's case, one of her contracts stipulates that call time is determined "at the sole discretion of the employer." This is a major red flag. Basically, it means that if the hospital happens to lose a surgeon, she may suddenly find herself on call every second or third night, versus the standard five.

BOLD PRINT

When reviewing a contract for the first time, pay close attention to passages in bold print. Once, while considering a new job, I guessed—correctly—that the parts of the contract in bold print were the items they expected to negotiate. After asking for a follow-up conversation, I looked for every passage they had bolded and negotiated a better deal for each.

And guess what? I was successful.

This may seem counterintuitive. After all, boldface print suggests emphasis and certainty, right? In this case, it served to highlight terms they frequently negotiate with new hires. If I hadn't led with confidence and trust, I might never have tried to secure better terms for myself.

RECOGNIZE YOUR VALUE

Above all, recognize your own value. If you don't, no one else will. This means being willing to walk away if the offer doesn't meet your expectations.

Remember the mindset lesson from Chapter 3, and get over the idea that advocating for yourself makes you seem greedy, noncommittal, or unreliable. Keeping a collaborative but firm approach is a great way to set the tone for how you operate as an employed physician or partner.

Once again, lead with confidence and trust—both in yourself and in your potential employer—even as you're forming an opinion. These qualities reflect much more positively in your tone and posture than suspicion and insecurity. They help you maintain composure and rapport as you set the stage for employment.

With the right information and approach, you can make the best choice and negotiate the best possible outcome. That doesn't mean getting every detail exactly how you want it. As attorney Amanda Hill noted in the *BOSS* podcast, "pick your battles." More importantly, that doesn't guarantee you and your new job will live happily ever after.

In the end, no position is perfect. And no human is either, BOSS MD or no.

In the end, Julia opted for the surgical private practice. However, you may have already guessed that this new job will not solve all her problems. Yes, she was able to identify red flags and negotiate some terms she wanted. Now she's got her malpractice tail, great maternity leave (just in case!), and more direct influence over her clinical schedule.

Still, when switching to a different organization and practice model, she's bound to encounter new issues. Plus, like everyone, she brings her own beliefs and patterns with her.

While she found a job she feels invested in, it doesn't take long for her to wonder whether they're investing enough in her. Specifically, in terms of helping her fill her clinic.

As a resident, you were trained to treat patients, not to get them in the door. It's normal to struggle with marketing your practice, especially at first, when you're still developing confidence as an attending physician.

This confidence curve can also impact your interpersonal dynamics when it comes to advocating for yourself and navigating difficult communications. Part 2 will help you express yourself and build autonomy through self promotion, relationship management, group dynamics, advocacy, and lobbying.

NEXT STEPS

1. List what you want from any contract. Have all new agreements written into your contract.
2. Secure your exit. Does the contract reflect fair termination procedures? Would it restrict your ability to practice near home? Does it provide tail coverage?
3. Check your mindset before and after interviews. Do you feel confident or insecure? Are you asking for what you want—and if not, why not? Reach out to a coach (like me!) to examine and release/replace limiting thoughts.
4. Before signing, have an attorney review your contract to protect your personal and professional interests.

BOSS PODCAST EPISODES:

https://www.BOSSsurgery.com/podcasts/
boss-business-of-surgery-series

Ep. 44: *Normalizing Negotiation, with Michael Johnson Jr., Esq, Physician Contract Lawyer*

Ep. 45: *Guard Your Practice, with Amanda Hill, Esq.*

PART 2

FIND YOUR VOICE

CHAPTER 5

SELF PROMOTION

Julia's new surgical private practice follows an eat-what-you-kill model—a term that to Julia sounds unnecessarily brutal, especially given her "do no harm" Hippocratic oath. She learned that every partner is responsible for building and maintaining their own patient base. Then, they each earn 100 percent of their self-generated revenues, minus overhead expenses.

Julia didn't worry too much about it at first, since she started with a one-year fixed salary to help her get on her feet. Now, a year and a half in, she's beginning—once again—to feel overwhelmed and under-supported.

Sometimes she easily fills her clinic. Toward the end of the calendar year, after more people have met their yearly deductibles, elective surgeries dominate her schedule. Now, in mid-January, it's nearly empty. So how do her more experienced partners keep more consistent patient followings?

Eat what you kill, huh? she thinks. *How are we supposed to save lives if we're thinking like predators?*

Before long, Julia resents this model. With many of the same old administrative concerns still wearing her down, now she *also* has to worry about advertising her services—something she's never been trained to do. Lately, Julia feels more hunted than hunter, wondering if her partners are somehow colluding with administrators to "poach" potential patients from her.

REFRAME YOUR SELF TALK

Maybe you've been there. You look at your clinic schedule and realize you only have a couple patients booked for the day. This impacts your reimbursement, triggering concerns about advancement and security.

Not to mention paranoia. You start wondering why the partner a few years ahead of you seems to get all the referrals. Why aren't admins helping *you* more? Before long, you view partners as competitors and administrators as potential enemies. Not exactly the story you want to write as a BOSS MD.

Drop this narrative. Instead, examine how you feel about marketing. Does something in you resist the act of self-promotion? If so, don't judge yourself; just get curious. What's that about? These questions speak to insecurities we all have. Namely that we're not good enough—and other people should be doing more for us.

The real question is: Are these stories even true?

In this chapter—indeed this whole book—we're going to dissect and hopefully discard the idea that our struggles are someone else's fault. Yes, sometimes people do bad things. Some systems truly are not fair. I'll even concede that sometimes, some people truly may even be out to "get" us.

The vast majority of the time? We're just spinning fictions about what other people are thinking and doing—and what they *should* be thinking or doing instead. When we do that, we become the ones pitting other people against *us*.

I'm not saying "blame yourself." That's a shame trap, so let's look instead for *solutions* when it comes to promoting yourself and your practice.

Above all, drop the assumption that just because you worked really hard to become a doctor, people should magically know who you are and what you do. You've earned your white coat, but you still have to earn your patient following.

CHECK YOUR RESISTANCE

As a new attending, you'll take on administrative duties you weren't expecting, don't yet fully understand, and aren't yet very good at—including marketing yourself. Rather than asking, "Why should I have to do this extra work?" recognize that you now have the opportunity to build something all your own. Then, accept that things start slow and build organically over time—including your own learning curve.

Too often, we expect others to do things for us—or at the very least, provide the validation or even permission we think we need to do things for ourselves. But meanwhile, everyone else is focused on building their own practices.

So we compare our journey to theirs. We end up resenting more experienced colleagues, because we think they should be giving their patients to us. We question whether we're good enough, making it even harder to promote ourselves.

It's normal to harbor doubts, even about mastery over clinical skills you've demonstrated over and over again. After years of "proving yourself worthy" of the mantle of MD or DO, you're not in the habit of saying, "I'm a great physician; everyone come to my clinic!"

As a resident, you may have asked a busy attending for a letter of recommendation, only to hear, "Why don't you write it yourself, then give it to me to look over?" If so, how hard was it for you to draft a positive self review?

Are you waiting for other people to notice your achievements, to affirm and promote you? Then it's time to recognize your own value, and speak it out loud.

EMBRACE THE OPPORTUNITY

Even in an eat-what-you-kill model, administrators do conduct some marketing for the practice, but that only takes you as far as the variable return on investment (ROI) of a billboard or website. By embracing your own professional marketing, you empower yourself to really grow.

On the *BOSS* podcast, I've talked to physicians who innovate creative, successful—and easy—self-promotion on Tik Tok, Instagram, and other digital platforms. Hospital administrators aren't likely to do something like that.

Sure, it's possible that patients are preferentially booked into a particular doctor's clinic, but that doesn't mean your admin is playing favorites. Patients often request a specific physician based on past personal experience, a recommendation from someone they know, or online reviews. Beyond that, they may have demographic preferences like male or female, or a shared language or cultural heritage. There may also be a problem in how you're listed in a physician directory (more on this below, under "Referral Patterns").

A lot of the disparity has to do with returning patients. Patients typically want to see the same person for continuity of care. Still, overbooked physicians sometimes ask administrators to schedule their returning patients to a new partners' clinic instead.

I've seen physicians who struggle with this in different ways. Most complain when their partners "don't share" patients, but I've also coached those who resent when admin gives them "other people's patients."

My response? "They're not other people's patients anymore. Now, they're yours."

Your patients—regardless of who they are or how they got there—are your best advocates to grow your practice. Every time you interact with a patient, you're tapping your best marketing strategy. If you can make that patient happy, they will spread the word.

YOUR MOST VALUABLE ASSETS

When it comes to specific marketing strategies, the landscape changes rapidly. Today's top social media platforms may be replaced within five years. That's why your best resource is always the patient in front of you.

It literally doesn't matter who ends up in your clinic or how. Make them happy, and they'll become evangelists for you.

Bring a clean, focused mind to your clinic. Treat every patient with the best care you possibly can. Not in a creepy, indulgent, linger-forever kind of way. Simply recognize the value, needs, and concerns of each individual. Their positive reviews—to family, friends, or online—represent exponential value when it comes to growing your practice.

ORGANIC MARKET RESEARCH

In terms of market research, your best resource is—surprise!—your patients themselves. Ask them things like, "How did you hear about our practice? Did anything in particular draw you to my clinic?"

Next, maximize their experience to not only keep them coming back, but also spread the word to family and friends through word of mouth, or publicly through an online review site.

Start by getting to know your current population's habits. Some, especially older demographics within smaller communities, still use traditional media sources. I recently had an older patient come in with an ad for our practice cut out from a newspaper.

Once you've asked enough patients, you'll see where you should concentrate your efforts.

Once you've learned how your patients get information, try something—literally anything—and see what happens. Maybe set up an Instagram account for your practice offering health tips or quick profiles of your support staff, then see if that builds any traction. Become a student of the process, because best practices change over time and vary by location.

In addition to asking patients outright, you can include an optional digital survey sent to their email address or via text. A lot of people may delete or ignore it—and that's okay—but some will fill it out. The results can provide feedback into how they found you and what kind of experience they had. With patient permission, this may also provide a way to mine anonymous testimonials for your website.

It helps to prepare patients. "After you leave, you'll get a text about rating your experience," you can say. "You don't have to do it, but if you're happy with this experience, it really helps me out if you leave a review."

Every time a new patient mentions positive reviews about me, I say, "Did you know that's how most people find new physicians? If you also have a positive experience here, it would help my practice—and the next person—if you would also consider sharing."

If patients give you direct positive feedback, thank them for the kind words and remind them that you're accepting new patients and it would really help if they shared more publicly what they just shared with you.

Make it as easy as possible by telling patients which physician review websites to check out. Monitor your online reviews and rotate recommendations accordingly. If your Healthgrades.com profile is saturated with reviews, suggest they go to Vitals.com, RateMDs.com, or whatever patient review site serves you best. If you've truly taken the time to develop an authentic relationship and provide the best possible care, many patients will want to help you in return.

Finally, don't stress too much over a "bad" review. Most patients are savvy enough to filter the odd (inevitable) complaint here or there. In fact, if there's an abundance of excellent reviews with only a few bad ones sprinkled in, your positive reviews will actually seem more valid.

REFERRAL PATTERNS

I'm a general surgeon, so my practice website used to describe me as such—without listing the range of surgeries I do. At first I assumed people would understand that a general surgeon can do things like breast cancer surgery, but people don't necessarily know that unless I tell them.

Meanwhile, in my same area, there was a gentleman specializing only in breast surgery. Because his physician directory spelled that out, he may have seemed like the only choice in town.

Make sure that on your website—or better yet, on multiple websites—you proactively list out the different kinds of care you offer or would like to do more of, as well as the geographic areas you serve. That way, when people put words into a search engine, they find you.

After adjusting my online physician bio, I went further. I reached out to primary care physicians and general surgeons in the area to let them know I'm an experienced breast surgeon interested in treating more breast cancer patients. All of a sudden—based on referrals from these physicians—more people started coming.

Those new patients were happy with the care they received, resulting in positive reports to their primary care doctors. Later, I ran into a family medicine friend who'd been referring patients to me.

"My patients were so happy with you," he said. "How else can I help support your practice? I just need to know what you do so I know who to send."

CENTER YOUR PATIENT CARE

One common mistake is focusing too much on personal achievements and credentials. No one cares about your degrees. They want to know whether or not you care about them and can help them.

Shift from "Look what I can do" to "What can I do for you?" Find out what each patient needs and how you personally can fill that need. Then tell them: "I see you're looking for X, and you're in the right place."

By making your self-promotion patient centered, you can better reframe this new responsibility: You're not competing with your colleagues or at odds with your hospital. You're all here to serve the same goal.

Julia can either continue to resent her empty clinic and spin a victim narrative around that...or she could reach out to the colleague currently outpacing her and find out what they're doing differently. Should she choose the latter, she may learn that this surgeon also struggled at first when building a patient following. Over time, he built symbiotic relationships with local primary care physicians—along with the courage to ask happy patients to leave positive online reviews.

In other words, her partner may have good advice to implement—but Julia's unlikely to ask for his insights as long as she views him as a threat. The next chapter dives deeper into repairing and improving difficult interpersonal relationships.

NEXT STEPS

1. Write a letter of reference for yourself. Examine any resistance to this exercise.
2. Write down any limiting beliefs you have about self promotion. Alone or with a coach, challenge the validity and cost of each.
3. Find out who referred new patients and send letters of appreciation.
4. Alert current patients when you're accepting new ones. Encourage them to tell friends and family. Explain where and how they can review your practice online.

5. Figure out which social media platforms your patients use and commit to posting there regularly—ideally once a week or more—providing public health tips relevant to your field and occasional practice updates.

BOSS PODCAST EPISODES:

https://www.BOSSsurgery.com/podcasts/
boss-business-of-surgery-series

Ep. 31: _Changing Jobs and Marketing for Yourself, with Dr. Bethany Malone_

Ep. 34: _Getting Patients into Clinic by Supporting PCPs, with Dr. Sarah Lee-Davisson_

Ep. 36: _Making Patients Evangelists (Raving Fans), with Dr. Brad Block_

Ep. 50: _Getting More Buy-In through Crafting a Powerful Message, with Dr. Dena George_

CHAPTER 6

RELATIONSHIP MANAGEMENT

Julia's partner Robert has worked at the practice for nearly a decade, and she increasingly finds him hot-headed, argumentative, and just…*smug*. He cuts her off during meetings and seems to knee-jerk object to all her recommendations. It's gotten to where she braces herself each time she sees him coming— including this morning.

"Hi, Julia," he says. "Not too busy today?"

What does he mean by that? Julia wonders before defensively spitting out, "Well, it's a slow time of year." As she walks away, she feels flustered. *Why would he rub my face in the fact that my clinic has slowed down?*

Julia knows that Robert's friendly with one of the administrators who helps schedule clinics. *I wonder what he says to her about me? Maybe that's why I'm not getting as many patients.*

Sure, his comment seems innocuous, but Robert and Julia have had moments—especially during staff meetings—where they've blatantly clashed. Julia's not used to having to fight for air time or defend each suggestion she makes. In fact, with tensions mounting, she's starting to wonder if the environment is getting too toxic for her to stay.

NOTICE YOUR RESPONSE

We've all had challenging work relationships. It could be a partner who pushes your buttons by downplaying your achievements or challenging everything you say. Maybe you have an administrator who creates extra work for you, or a supervisor who takes credit for your work.

If someone repeatedly rankles you, your autonomic nervous system may recast them as a threat. You start to see the relationship through a lens of self-protection. Each time you encounter this person, your body remembers past interactions and instinctively prepares for battle.

Suddenly, you're interpreting neutral comments—"You've picked up another patient"—as some cryptic, antagonistic dig.

If you're getting flustered before even saying hello, you're likely to feed the tension and perpetuate misunderstandings. This leads to negative thought spirals that further catastrophize the situation. You may get to the point where you consider leaving an otherwise good job over one unpleasant interpersonal relationship.

First, dial down your body's automatic response. When you feel triggered, your body defaults to a trauma response. This is not to equate a negative work relationship with full-on trauma, only that something about it reminds your brain of previous times when you've felt threatened. Maybe this coworker reminds you of a toxic ex or relative.

For our purposes, unpacking the history of your personal triggers is less important than recognizing and responding to your body's signals. We're all a product of our past experiences, and our brains want to keep us safe by activating fight, flight, or freeze mode. That's why our cheeks flush or shoulders tense before we can even reply. If we don't learn to mindfully manage perceived threats, we will automatically respond through the primitive brain's survival mechanism.

When you're not actually in danger—but you nevertheless respond from a triggered state—the response comes across as dysfunctional, creating worse problems. Now, you're more likely to trigger someone else's unconscious trauma. Perhaps this coworker's autonomic nervous system associates your snippy reply with negative past interactions of his own. Maybe you're now playing the role of *his* overbearing ex in the movie he's playing in his head.

ACCEPT AND EXAMINE YOUR TRIGGER

First of all, recognize that this whole thing is completely normal and nothing to feel ashamed about. Sometimes we find we're more afraid of what a trigger "means about us" than we are of the situation itself. At the end of the day, though, it's just an autonomic response everyone has.

It can help to take a moment to thank your mind and body for trying to keep you safe. Then, take a deep breath, and remind yourself that you're not actually in danger. Finally, get curious about the situation.

Do not try to avoid your triggers. You probably don't have to change your entire career trajectory because of one difficult colleague. In fact, the best way to address and overcome triggers is to actually seek them out. Trauma responses point us to something we need to look at—where work is needed. Rather than some indictment of why we're "bad" or "doing it wrong," identifying triggers can provide a gateway to freedom.

Here's a personal example. Lately, each time I sit down to work on this book you're reading, my brain shuts down. Before I committed to writing a book, I could effortlessly type out my thoughts and observations.

I now have a choice: I could make this freeze response mean that I can't write a book because I'm a terrible writer with nothing worthwhile to share. Or, I could recognize that I'm just having a fear response. Then, I could ask, "What am I afraid of? What belief do I have about what might go wrong—and what is that costing me?"

Finally, I can task myself with a manageable goal: First I'll finish this sentence, then I'll outline the rest of Chapter 6—to tackle tomorrow.

VISUALIZATION TECHNIQUES

When we perceive a person (or book chapter) as a threat, we know we're more likely to react in an avoidant or otherwise dysfunctional way. One way to neutralize the perceived threat is by planning ahead—before the encounter—for how we'll think about the situation.

Reframing your thoughts about a person or activity in advance can dial down the autonomic response. When you come into a situation having rehearsed that the other person is a villain you must protect yourself from, all you've done is feed that story. It's now more likely to unfold as an antagonistic exchange.

When the conversation feels fraught with friction, you lean into confirmation bias: *See?! I knew he had it in for me.* Meanwhile, since we're not conscious of our internal filter, we struggle to clearly and objectively observe the situation.

Maybe, all that person's doing is walking down the hall making small talk.

You can use your imagination for good or ill, so let's try a different tactic. Try visualizing the person in a non-threatening way. Just like in Chapter 3—when we discussed visualizing your job interviewer in their undies—it helps to pick something comical, or even a bit outrageous.

Imagine the person dressed in a full on clown suit, in one of those inflatable dinosaur costumes, or anything else that brings a smile to your face. If, like Julia's colleague, the person's a bit of a hothead, you might imagine his adult head on a toddler's body throwing a fit. One client I coached imagined his coworker as an angry ferret running around the meeting room. Just make sure it's a non-threatening vision (if you're terrified of the movie *It*, skip the clown suit.)

To better appreciate the power of imagination, consider a concept from the Harry Potter series. In J.K. Rowling's fiction, shadowy creatures called dementors keep prisoners trapped by literally consuming their hope and life force. The characters know when dementors are near because they suddenly feel colder and weaker.

Similarly, whenever a difficult colleague walks into the conference room, you may instinctively shiver and tense up. If you take the bait and spend the meeting arguing with thtem, you'll leave flustered and drained. However, once you realize you've created—or at least fed—the dementor image in your own head, you can plan ahead, check your response, and stop freely giving away your life force.

While we're on the topic, there's another interesting Harry Potter creature called a boggart, a magical entity that physically embodies your worst fear. The spell for disarming this shape-shifter involves re-visualizing the boggart. For example, the wizard-in-training Neville most fears the intimidating Professor Snape. However, once he imagines boggart-as-Snape wearing his grandmother's clothes, the entire class starts laughing, and the boggart loses power.

It all comes down to harnessing your imagination—the stories and beliefs you rehearse in your head. Then, get curious. Experiment by allowing yourself to reframe and reinterpret the situation.

ADJUST YOUR COMMUNICATION

Once you calm your autonomic response, you can better adjust how you engage with the person. Let's revisit some job interview tricks from Chapter 3.

When engaging with someone you find triggering, find ways to build in pauses—especially if they say or do something that ordinarily sets you off. Rather than knee-jerk reacting to something objectionable, simply take a beat.

Breathe.

Then try mirroring. Repeat back the last thing they said in the form of a neutral question. This way, without agreeing or disagreeing, you've bought yourself some time and space to think.

The biggest difference between the difficult colleague and the job interview is that, in the case of the former, you have more history (and future) with this person. Since the stakes may feel higher, it's even more important to dial down that autonomic response.

By employing pauses and mirroring phrases, you retrain your brain to slow down and engage in more mindful communications. Now, you're less likely to turn them into the fearful "boggart" of your unconscious fears and more likely to objectively perceive the situation—right here, right now—for what it is.

Sometimes, the person notices the difference in your demeanor and also relaxes. Plus, this approach increases your ability to fully listen. Even if the person still argues or cuts you off, don't react right away. The first time or two, it may feel like you're losing ground or letting yourself be steamrolled. However, by not feeding the negative pattern, you will begin grounding yourself in your own power.

After all, why argue with someone who's committed to misunderstanding you? By keeping your cool, you can preserve your sanity—and others are more likely to perceive you as in command.

How could Julia have responded differently to the comment, "Not too busy today?" Once she'd dialed down her autonomic response, given herself a pause, and considered what was really said (rather than what she thought she heard), she could have employed some humor: "Never too busy for coffee!"

Each interaction is one step closer to mastery—whether we learn from perceived "failures" or from signs of progress, no matter how small.

SEEK VALIDATION WITHIN

After practicing these visualization and communication skills, my coaching clients often report higher energy levels and better relationships at work. Once you stop feeding negative stories and reacting to everything, you realize how much energy and power you unconsciously give away.

A lot of this comes down to external validation-seeking rooted in an irrational fear about how other people perceive you. Most of the time, we misinterpret how—and how often—other people think about us. Plus, it's truly none of our business. Simply make it okay for other people to misunderstand or disagree, and suddenly it becomes a lot easier to authentically express yourself.

We often get so attached to our victim-villain stories that we want other people to affirm when we believe we're being treated unfairly. However, in the case of a challenging colleague, creating a more functional work dynamic is far more important than validating some story you've been telling yourself about "right" and "wrong."

In the end, validation-seeking behavior exposes our own insecurities without resolving them. This may be rooted in how we were treated by our parents as a child. Suddenly, we're internalizing a deep-seated story about self-worth and projecting that onto an irrelevant grown-up situation.

The vast majority of interpersonal dynamics are determined by inner states. This means that, as the BOSS MD protagonist of your own story, you have a lot more influence over relationships than you think—as long as you approach the situation mindfully, rather than filtering everything through your autonomic primitive brain.

I can recognize elements of Julia's avoidant behavior in my own resistance to wrapping up this chapter. However, as author, I have the power to reframe not only my own story, but also hers.

So let's shift the narrative. Suppose Julia begins to realize that—just maybe—she doesn't have to object or compete every time Robert takes over a meeting. After building in pauses, she finds that she simply doesn't care as much about how he behaves or what he says. She takes responsibility for her own self-validation, rather than insisting that Robert reflect anything in particular back to her.

Before long, when Julia does speak up, her input carries more weight. After one such interaction, a surgery resident privately thanks Julia for so calmly standing up for a particular point. Far from needing to leave the practice, Julia realizes she can repair a difficult relationship through small internal shifts.

Now that she's stopped comparing herself to and needing something from her gruff older colleague, Julia can see how much influence she truly has—especially regarding how younger colleagues view her. People really are paying attention—if not in the way she thought. She was too busy worrying about how difficult partners and administrators viewed her to see how she has positively impacted her workplace.

Like Julia, you will navigate challenging work relationships. Once you move beyond internalized doubt and externalized blame, you can achieve more mindful and productive dynamics. The next chapter takes this lesson about one-on-one interactions a step further by applying it within the context of group interactions.

NEXT STEPS

1. When dealing with people who trigger you, identify thoughts or beliefs that prompt or reinforce this response.
2. Create strategies to dial down your autonomic system through visualization techniques or working with a coach.
3. Imagine a trainee or colleague you'd like to inspire. How would you want them to respond during difficult interactions? When you get triggered, keep that person in mind, rather than focusing on your "adversary."

BOSS PODCAST EPISODES:

https://www.BOSSsurgery.com/podcasts/
boss-business-of-surgery-series

Ep. 3: *The Difficult Partner Webinar Replay*

Ep. 59: *Feeling Safe at Work*

Ep. 65: *Medicine, Marriage and Money, with Dr. Kate Mangona*

Ep. 18: *Life without Limits and Gaslighting, with Dr. Julie Riley*

Ep. 68: *When the Wrong Job Is Hurting You, with Dr. Sara Rasmussen*

CHAPTER 7

GROUP DYNAMICS

Like most people, Julia looks forward to Fridays. Not because it starts the weekend (she's often on call then too), but because that's when she spends all day in the operating room. No meetings. No paperwork or admin. Just a full day of doing what she loves.

Until now. Opening her email this Monday morning, Julia reads a message alerting her that, starting this week, her Friday OR block will be chopped in half. Instead of eight hours, the practice will only cover four.

Julia nearly spits out her coffee. "What is going on!?" she shouts to an empty kitchen. Immediately, her mind starts spiraling through questions (mostly variations on *Why is this happening to me?*)

She feels furious and powerless. During her commute, she spins conspiracy theories about partners stealing time and administrative disrespect.

At their Monday partner check in, Julia's still grinding through various interrelated grievances. At first, she quietly fumes to avoid lashing out, followed by a somewhat tense exchange with her senior partner that—in Julia's mind—resolves nothing.

PROCESSING VERSUS INDULGING EMOTIONS

In the last chapter, we talked about how to stop your primitive brain from hijacking the system when faced with a difficult interpersonal relationship. This chapter takes it a step further, applying similar principles within broader group dynamics. Mainly, we'll discuss how to respond effectively to administrative forces that influence your career and day-to-day work.

As we've seen, most of becoming the BOSS MD is an inside job. Yes, you'll have supervisors, schedules, and other administrative pressures to deal with—and you cannot control every outcome. However, if you take full command over how you respond, you better communicate your needs and influence how things get run.

First of all, your negative feelings are valid. They often stem from a situation—whether real or perceived—in which your needs have not been met. Even when they stem from an honest misunderstanding, feelings should be honored, examined, and processed.

However, there's a big difference between processing emotions and indulging them. When we feel overwhelmed or disrespected, our bodies default to that autonomic nervous system response. In other words, we may freak out, which doesn't provide much direction for moving forward.

In her book *The Gifts of Imperfection*, author Brené Brown recommends asking yourself two questions:

1. Do I have enough information to be freaking out? (Probably not.)
2. Will freaking out help? (Nope.)

Don't get me wrong. You still have to process the fight-flight-flee hormones coursing through your body. If you can, walk away from the person or situation that catalyzed your response. Take some deep breaths. Move your body. If you can, maybe shout into a pillow or hit a punching bag.

Pay close attention to what your brain does next. Does it grind through stories of past wrongs? Are you rehearsing arguments and fortifying beliefs of unfairness, mistreatment, and oppression?

Psychologists tend to agree that anger functions as a secondary emotion covering up something else, like overwhelm, betrayal, or (most often) some kind of fear. When you *feed* that anger, whether through rumination or endless imagined conversations with other people, not only are you not resolving the underlying emotion; you're adding accelerant to that emotion, fueling your own spinout.

Then, you're more likely to lash out, escalate tensions, and regret it later. Not only did you not identify and address the underlying feeling or issue, now you've also got a tertiary emotion of shame or embarrassment about how you dealt with it all. This is especially true for women, who are often judged more harshly for expressing anger.

In Julia's case, she applied a certain meaning (i.e., disrespect, injustice, powerlessness) to her surprise schedule change. This colored her approach to the staff meeting, which she interpreted as some high stakes conflict. As a result, it didn't go so well, which only confirmed her bias and reinforced her mood, creating an environment even less conducive to cooperation.

We want to show up in a helpful way, so how do we get there? What's the best route from disaffection and disagreement to a place where everyone's voice is heard and "everything's negotiable"?

DIG DOWN TO THE ROOTS

Again, it starts with examining your stories. Powerlessness may be one story you've been telling yourself. When you're committed to that (or any) story, you can and will make it true for yourself.

As we discussed in Chapter 1, over time our thoughts become the building blocks of our beliefs. Since we've built them ourselves, we can also break them down. By consciously choosing different thoughts, we can start believing something different.

Anger is a bitter fruit that often stems from fear, combined with a sense of powerlessness. In reality, you are far more powerful than you think. Your voice is valuable, and you can affect the outcome.

If you don't like what happened to your schedule, you can address the situation and try to do something about it. But first, you need to dig to the root of the situation. You're not going to negotiate effectively unless the other person senses that you also understand their needs, fears, and goals.

Rather than walking in with guns blazing, come ready to listen. The impulse to "win" makes it harder to accurately gather information, let alone identify underlying issues, common goals, and potential solutions. It helps to accept in advance that you may not get the response or support you want. This reduces pressure, making it easier to observe and understand what's going on.

Every party has their own needs and motivations. If we speak only to what we see on the surface level, we miss the deeper point. At home, you may feel frustrated with your child for not unloading the dishwasher. You could rant about clean dishes all day—or, you could point out that when you have to continually remind them to help with chores, you feel unsupported and disrespected. Chances are, no one's deliberately trying to make you feel this way. Expressing this underlying feeling can help others see you without feeding into their own defenses.

Both at home and at work, get curious about conflict. Try to objectively figure out what the underlying need, fear, or concern may be, then speak to that level instead.

Your hospital may want to cut back on cancer treatment patients because they only see the amount of money it costs to conduct cancer-related surgeries. If you identify this underlying concern, there may be a different way to address the issue.

Perhaps you can point out the downstream effects. Fewer cancer surgeries may reduce the amount of money the hospital would receive for chemotherapy, radiation, or additional studies. While they were looking at only one metric, you could provide other details that demonstrate bigger-picture financials related to accepting cancer patients.

In other words, rather than assuming "they're just jerks," try on the idea that administrators may not know what you know. I find that, if I'm going to make assumptions, it's usually more helpful (and accurate) to err on the side of generosity.

That said, it takes time to adjust and apply this new perspective. While defensiveness easily becomes automatic, generosity can require more deliberate, conscious thought.

LISTEN, THEN SPEAK UP

At Julia's practice, they've taken OR time away from her, which feels scary because she's worried about money. Meanwhile, they've probably made this choice based on their own budget concerns.

Once Julia understands this, she can speak to that level, then offer her perspective. It certainly doesn't help to immediately get defensive or argue about what is or isn't "true." That just leads to competing narratives.

Start by listening. Force yourself to quiet down and truly consider the other side. This requires looking past your own unmet need. It also means deactivating—if momentarily—the part of you that disagrees with the other person. This can be really, really hard to do.

But if you do it right, not only will you better understand where they're coming from, they'll also be a lot more likely to negotiate. Why? It all goes back to tactical empathy (per Chapter 3). People feel more inclined to work with someone who listens to and validates their underlying concerns.

Next, speak to those concerns. Julia may learn they're cutting her surgery block because her clinic has slowed down. However, she sees something they don't see. Administrators may have established this time block utilization based on flawed information. Now—as long as she doesn't get defensive and spin out—she may be able to negotiate a return to her eight-hour Friday block, provided she brings in more surgery patients within the next month.

Physicians get so swamped by their day-to-day duties they often fail to appreciate what goes into management decisions. There are real people behind every business decision, so find the administrators or committees involved and speak directly to them. Not to file a complaint per se, but to learn more about what's going on and why.

This helps you dip your toes into leadership dynamics beyond your own clinic. By showing consideration for challenges administrators face, you get involved and begin to influence outcomes—without giving up what you most love about medicine.

You can show up and be heard—it's on you to listen first, then speak up. You're far more likely to get what you want by cooperatively arriving at a mutually beneficial solution, rather than leaning into all-or-nothing thinking.

LEADERSHIP

As Julia becomes more cognizant of her beliefs and behavioral patterns, she speaks up more—after understanding where others are coming from, and with less attachment to specific outcomes.

When she doesn't like a particular management decision, she now acknowledges that other humans made that choice—and not because they're determined to make her miserable. She can find those humans and listen to what they have to say, then use her voice and expertise to feel out other options.

Of course, she won't win every time, often because she doesn't know the whole picture. But by showing up for herself and others—by listening first, then using her voice—she can improve outcomes for herself and others.

This approach can become a self-fulfilling prophecy. Even when she can't immediately change the outcome, if Julia addresses the issue with calm self-assurance, she's more likely to gain ground down the road. Meanwhile, she sets an empowering example for younger colleagues.

Once Julia calms down and gets out of her way, she can approach her senior partner again—this time to truly listen, then more effectively advocate for herself and come to some collaborative agreement moving forward. With this approach, she can even reclaim her Friday surgery block, provided she more consistently fills her clinic.

From patient care to staff meetings, group dynamics sometimes get messy and heated. If you consistently show up in a spirit of true collaboration, you'll eventually make a positive impact on the culture around you. Part of your professional evolution is learning to exert influence within your practice, and maybe even more broadly within the medical industry. It all starts within.

NEXT STEPS

1. List your thoughts and beliefs regarding your role within different groups at work. Interrogate the accuracy and costs of those thoughts and beliefs.
2. Find out who makes what decisions in your organization and what factors they consider.
3. Step outside your comfort zone in meetings. If you over-share or talk over others, challenge yourself to stay quiet and actively listen. If you're shy, speak up more.

BOSS PODCAST EPISODES:

https://www.BOSSsurgery.com/podcasts/
boss-business-of-surgery-series

Episode 8: *Admin Is Not the Enemy*

Episode 37: *Are You Working with a Bad Leader? with Dr. Kenneth Cho*

Ep. 70: *Leadership Lessons from the Advisory Board, with Dr. Sarah Lee-Davisson and Dr. Beth Avena*

Ep. 15: *Rising the Ranks with Self-less Leadership, with Dr. AJ Copeland*

CHAPTER 8

ADVOCACY

Julia's gaining more autonomy and influence at work. She's standing up for herself, mentoring herself, and educating younger colleagues. As she gains more bandwidth in her career, she feels more agency and sense of purpose—not to mention a greater appreciation of how the medical system could improve.

Julia often sees fundraising posts on social media about disease research and sometimes gets emails from the American Medical Association about lobbying Congress over surprise medical bills. She's beginning to wonder if she should somehow make a bigger difference within her field.

Once people begin empowering themselves, they often feel called to do more. While protesting on Capitol Hill or starting a social media awareness campaign are both noble enterprises, not everyone is cut out for formal advocacy—and that's okay.

While this chapter highlights examples of low-effort, high-impact advocacy campaigns, it mainly explores how you can make a difference at work and within your community in small but impactful ways every single day—without the hashtags or marches.

FORMAL ADVOCACY

Let's begin with examples of successful physician activism. We'll explore both a smaller, community effort to raise money for disease research and treatment, as well as a national safety campaign related to a highly politicized issue.

MULTIPLE SCLEROSIS

Dr. Maura Lipp works as an intensive care unit doctor in my current home base of Columbia, Tennessee. A few years ago, she noticed uncomfortable burning and tingling sensations in her extremities, plus growing pain in her eyes, head, and upper back. Before long, she suffered occasional muscle spasms, vertigo, and blurred vision.

On receiving a diagnosis for multiple sclerosis, Dr. Lipp responded with straight-up denial. Afraid of what it might say about her competence as a physician, she initially refused to acknowledge the diagnosis to herself, let alone disclose it to others.

It took time for Dr. Lipp to mentally reconcile her self-image of the invulnerable, overachieving ICU doctor with the hand she'd been dealt. Once she was able to accept her circumstances and seek the help she needed, she found ways to better manage the symptoms while preserving her career and reputation.

Soon, she began wondering how many others silently struggle with multiple sclerosis. She realized that, as a physician living with the condition, she has a unique opportunity to offer perspective, encouragement, and treatment options.

In 2019, Dr. Lipp launched a local group to educate and support both diagnosed individuals and their families and friends. She facilitated the group with the help of the chaplain at the regional non-profit health system where she worked.

She created an environment for open discussion, group support, and information about resources related to MS. Meanwhile, her community group raised hundreds of thousands in grants to fund research and treatment.

This story speaks to the power of internal shifts. First, Dr. Lipp looped through insecurity, denial, and near-despair. However, once she became more compassionate with herself, she stopped resisting what she couldn't change. She accepted her feelings and took care of her needs. This freed up energy and focus, empowering her to help others as well.

"OUR LANE"

Joseph Sakran was seventeen years old when a stray bullet pierced his neck. He was at a playground after a high school football game when a fellow teenager fired at a rival and hit Sakran instead. Despite emergency surgery that saved his life, he incurred permanent damage to one of his vocal cords.

He went on to become a trauma surgeon at Johns Hopkins and founder of the now-famous Twitter handle @ThisIsOurLane, which evolved into a movement uniting medical professionals to advocate for gun violence prevention and research.

Dr. Sakran's digital activism began in 2018, after the American College of Physicians publicly released a position paper recommending a public health approach to reducing firearm deaths and injuries—in response to which, the National Rifle Association tweeted that doctors should "stay in their lane," suggesting that trauma surgeons had no business weighing in.

This inspired an outpouring of surgeons and other physicians sharing stories related to the public health impact of gun violence—including Dr. Sakran, who quickly emerged as a leader of the movement.

LEADING THROUGH EXPERIENCE

Injury and illness strike doctors too. When this happens, we can ask ourselves: "Why me?" Or we can accept what happened and embrace our power to help both ourselves and others.

If we face politicized resistance, we have options. Dr. Sakran could have easily raged and villainized the other point of view. Having experienced first-hand the devastating impact of permissive gun legislation, he might be justified in lashing out, engaging endlessly with the NRA's arguments, and accusing them of politically and financially motivated propaganda.

Instead, his approach was more measured. Dr. Sakran remained calm and direct, focusing his message on his related personal experience and expertise. As physicians, we're uniquely qualified to centralize what we know, prioritizing the human perspective of the physician's experience.

ADVOCATING FOR OTHER DOCTORS

If you need any more evidence that we're our own heroes, I have plenty of examples to share (and it's impossible to name them all!). The following physicians all started with small steps, but they believed in their mission and in the possibility of change.

Dr. Jim Dahle created a simple blog, which turned into White Coat Investor, a multi-media company inspiring physicians to achieve financial freedom. https://www.whitecoatinvestor.com/

Dr. Kevin Pho, founder of KevinMD, began his online career with a book on social media for doctors, which transformed into the largest online platform for physicians to tell stories not often heard in medicine. https://www.kevinmd.com/

Dr. Hala Sabry created Physician Mom's Group, an online community of over 70K physicians. Her efforts to combat isolation and provide online support impacted countless individuals and inspired similar groups. https://mypmg.com/

Dr. Sunny Smith, founder of the program Empowering Women Physicians, pioneered the physician coaching revolution. As a founding physician coach, she has inspired hundreds of physicians to lend support on burnout, empowerment, financial freedom, and self-advocacy. https://empoweringwomenphysicians.com/

Dr. Una, founder of EntreMD, got our attention with her call: "The calvary is not coming…we are the calvary." She helps doctors create profitable businesses so they can live and practice medicine on their terms. Her thriving podcast, online business school, and retreats led to features in *Forbes* and *Inc.* https://entremd.com/

Dr. Heena Santry is a trauma surgeon who planned to become an academic chair and expand diversity, equity, and inclusion efforts. Upon realizing she might have greater impact outside of academia, she forged her own way. Like Hala Sabry, Dr. Santry created an online group of over 3K surgeon mothers who support each other through the challenges of being a woman in a historically male-dominated field.

These outstanding physicians are just like you and me. They saw the problems in medicine, and learned how to advocate for much-needed change.

MY BOSS MD MISSION

My personal mission is simply to dispel the myth that the right answer to physician burnout is leaving medicine.

Physicians often note that taking a leave of absence does not result in them feeling better. Trying to solve overworking by quitting does nothing to improve anyone's relationship to either work or self-worth. It only reinforces the notion that work is the problem.

Instead, I want to empower physicians to find small but powerful ways to better show up for themselves, their patients, and each other. I want them to embody the BOSS MD both at work and in life, rather than resenting everything wrong with our profession. When we take responsibility for our patterns of beliefs and behaviors, we can reframe our experience and re-engage in a more effective way.

This, I'm convinced, is how we change medicine for the better.

Perhaps, like Julia, you clash with certain colleagues and administrators at work. Or maybe you just feel overwhelmed and worn down by administrative demands. You may even rage against systemic injustices or unnecessary complications within our nation's medical system. At times, you may feel so hopeless that you're tempted to throw in the towel altogether.

There's so much negativity and injustice you have absolutely no control over. That said, there's also much you can do—both within your smaller sphere of influence and within your broader community—that improves not only your professional experience and trajectory, but also the system at large.

YOU HAVE OPTIONS

It may be something as small and mundane as choosing to leave a particularly dysfunctional workplace environment that clearly isn't going to change. As we explored in Chapter 2, you have more career options than you might think. Maybe you're not doing anything wrong; you're just in the wrong place.

I once coached someone dealing with an interpersonal conflict. Her supervisor sent her to a performance enhancement training, which she interpreted at the first step toward a layoff. She grew defensive and suspicious, obsessing over perceived clues that her job was doomed. At some point, she wondered if she was cut out for being a doctor at all.

After taking with me, she identified patterns of harmful office culture that had nothing to do with her. She also noticed ways that her own unexamined fears and beliefs impacted how she showed up at work, perpetuating unhelpful dynamics.

The more she worked on herself, the more she realized she didn't need to quit medicine—but perhaps she *did* need to leave that workplace culture. Realizing she had the power to seek a better professional fit helped calm her fears of being fired.

This client did end up finding a better job. But first, she spoke up for herself—calmly, without casting blame, and with much less attachment to the outcome.

On her way out, some of her colleagues thanked her. By gently and fearlessly voicing her concerns—and knowing when to walk—she highlighted long neglected problems with organizational culture. After others followed her lead to greener pastures, the executive leader responsible for much of the dysfunctional, outdated approach retired early.

All this woman did was stand up for herself, then make a life decision to better address her needs. However, the changes in her behavior and actions led to a broader positive cultural shift in the organization she left behind.

While you cannot change other people, you can influence them—by listening, speaking up when needed, and making the right choices for you.

Finally, if you're in a situation like this, it helps to consult your attorney about how to properly file a complaint or notice of wrongdoing before you leave. Setting yourself up for success means being strategic about what you report and how you quit. When you have to move on from a job, go with grace.

RIPPLE EFFECT

When political tensions—both at large and in the office—trigger personal outrage, you'll operate through a victim-villain lens. This may get you fired up (or simply fired), or it may cause you to despair. Either way, with this mentality, you're not likely to resolve anything, not for yourself or anyone else.

However, once you take responsibility for how you show up and interact with others, you can change your own relationships and influence broader culture. Your patterns of beliefs and actions directly impact your loved ones, your colleagues, and your patients—and indirectly, everyone *they* come into contact with.

Again, we cannot change others, but we can influence them—and influence is an inside job. Once you shift from victim to BOSS MD, you can positively impact dynamics around you—for yourself, the people you care for, and the community you serve.

It all ripples out from there.

This chapter highlighted examples of physicians organizing larger efforts to provide community support, amplify physician voices, and improve public health and safety. Perhaps you feel drawn to something similar. Or, you may wish to make a difference through medical education or mentorship.

That said, you don't have to start marching in DC, create a support group, or even apply for an academic position to advocate for positive change. You certainly don't have to shout at political opponents or force lobbying groups or strangers on Twitter to change their minds.

Once Julia began more consistently and skillfully showing up for herself and those around her, she made a positive impact on younger colleagues. Like her, start by examining stories you tell yourself, how you engage with those around you, and when to use your voice. This is your exponential effect.

That's not to say you must radiate positivity 24/7 and never make mistakes. In fact, recognizing and repairing what you get wrong can have an even greater impact than doing everything right.

Vulnerability takes courage, but sometimes the best you can do is admit your faults and even laugh at yourself. It's okay to not do everything perfectly. In fact, it's inevitable. Part three will explore in greater detail how we can improve outcomes, including the concept of the perfection trap.

NEXT STEPS

1. Ask yourself: If I knew I wouldn't fail, what steps would I take to change the world?
2. Explore what you tell yourself about your ability to create this change in the world.
3. Alone or with a coach, commit to one step that moves you toward this change.

BOSS PODCAST EPISODES:

https://www.BOSSsurgery.com/podcasts/
boss-business-of-surgery-series

Ep. 6: *#Speakup Ortho and Ending Residency Harassment and Bullying*

Ep. 11: *Advocacy and Leading a Purpose-Driven Life, with Dr. Joseph Sakran Thisisourlane*

Ep. 14: *Living Life and Practicing Medicine on Your Terms, with Dr. Una*

Ep. 20, pt. 2: *Fighting Insurance Companies and Becoming an Advocate with a Chronic Illness Diagnosis, with Dr. Maura Lipp*

Ep. 41: *From Burnout to Determined, with Dr. Jimmy Turner*

Ep. 28: *Health Care Design for Health Care Equity and Burnout Prevention, with Dr. Heena Santry*

Ep. 12: *Rise of the Physician Coach, with Dr. Sunny Smith, and Supporting the Henrietta Lacks Foundation*

PART 3

IMPROVE OUTCOMES

CHAPTER 9

COMPLICATIONS

Julia's sitting down to dinner when she gets the call. A patient she'd performed surgery on two days ago—who was initially doing well—now has a fever and elevated heart rate. "And worsening abdominal pain," the nurse adds.

This patient presented with colon cancer. Julia conducted emergency surgery to remove the entire affected intestinal section, then reconnected the bowel.

After arriving to clinic and confirming her suspicion of an anastomotic leak, Julia's own gut sinks. Had she made a mistake? This is Julia's (and everyone's) least favorite part of the job. Long accustomed to striving for perfection, complications grate at her, tightening her belly and shortening her fuse.

"Schedule a colostomy," Julia barks.

"On it," says the OR nurse.

To make matters worse, Robert—*Mr. Perfect Surgeon himself*— happens to be within earshot. "It's okay," he says (*flippantly*, Julia thinks). "He's gonna be fine."

"Thanks, but it's NOT okay," Julia snaps, excusing herself to the bathroom to collect her thoughts. As Julia already knows, in any complex, high-risk job, things go wrong. Unfortunately, she's now fallen prey to the perfection trap.

The perfection trap first loads us down with the unnecessary weight of impossible standards. Then it ties one hand behind our backs by making sure we never ask for help. This alone perpetuates anxiety and burnout, making complications more likely.

The worst part comes when things go wrong. When—not *if*— we face an imperfect outcome, perfectionism wants to *hide*. It casts us into a shame response. We feel terrible. We withdraw. Maybe we get angry at ourselves or lash out when colleagues try to reassure us. This chapter explores how to cultivate shame resilience in order to escape this perfection trap, resolve negative outcomes, learn, and move on.

THE PERFECTION TRAP

There are two broad categories of medical complications. Some result from huge, flagrant mistakes—say, accidentally leaving a foreign body inside a patient. Those are exceptionally rare, and this chapter won't deal with them. We all know not to stitch up a patient with an operator sponge in their abdomen.

Instead, we'll consider the far more likely and mundane version of complications, like the anastomotic leak following Julia's colon operation. When it comes to this far more common category, no physician has a zero percent failure rate. That's because no *procedure* has a zero percent failure rate—even when we do everything right.

You might expect surgery patients to take comfort in the thought that their attending is a perfectionist. With stakes that high, "failure is not an option" seems like the attitude you'd want in a surgeon.

The truth is that, in any complex, high-risk job, things go wrong. Mistakes happen in every setting and context, including the OR. And contrary to popular belief, perfectionism does exactly *nothing* to prevent this.

As physicians, we must accept our human fallibility. Not only will we make mistakes, but—like all humans—we're much more likely to err when we feel stressed. And guess what? Perfectionism creates *more stress*.

That's because it's rooted in shame, and shame is counterproductive at best. It wants us to self-isolate and punish ourselves. We reject outside support. We hear only criticism. We no longer look at the situation with the objective, dispassionate lens needed to understand what went wrong—let alone to fix the problem or prevent it from happening again.

You may have experienced times when shame or fear caused you to withdraw or lash out. If it becomes a pattern, this will alienate your colleagues. You may start resenting people who still seem "perfect." In extreme cases, it may lead you to job hop or switch careers altogether.

At this point in the perfection trap, you're actively seeking evidence to support the catastrophe narrative. You might misinterpret people's words, tones, or actions as proof. I've heard this storm of negative thoughts referred to as the "Itty Bitty Shitty Committee," offering all kinds of unhelpful ideas: *Now they know I'm not cut out for this. They won't want me here anymore. I should just leave.*

By the way—all of this is natural. It's 100 percent normal and okay to feel bad when you mess up. It shows you care about your patients. Besides, as aspiring physicians, we all learned to chase the perfect GPA and compete against other seemingly perfect overachievers for residency programs, then internships, then jobs.

If no one ever taught us about shame resilience, or how to avoid the perfection trap, it's probably because our attending physicians often struggled with this themselves.

Here's where the BOSS MD mindset comes in. While we can't completely avoid mistakes—or the emotions that come along with those—we *can* choose how to interpret the situation and act on it.

SHAME VERSUS GUILT

First: Accept that you will make mistakes at some point in your medical career.

Next: Accept that—as a highly trained, high achieving professional with functioning empathy—you will feel bad about it.

The trick is to process the experience as guilt, rather than letting yourself get carried away by shame. What's the difference? Guilt relates to something you've *done*. Because it's focused on actions, guilt is *actionable*.

You can address guilt through accountability and analysis. Admit to the mistake and figure out how it happened. Then, do what you can to resolve the issue and move on. While regrettable, you've now learned something from the experience—hopefully, how to avoid the problem moving forward.

Shame, on the other hand, wants to define *who you are*. By nature, shame is avoidant, reactive, and self-punishing. It's also *exhausting*. Not to mention delusional.

Because here's the thing: Patients don't actually expect us to be perfect.

RE-EXAMINE EXPECTATIONS

Let's start by getting your own expectations in order. First of all, expect to mess up at some point. Next, expect that you're not going to feel good about complications, mistakes, or any variety of imperfect outcomes.

Practice accepting this potential reality—before any mishaps occur. That will make it easier to avoid or recover from shame spirals, then move into actionable guilt when needed. Suddenly, you just feel bad about the situation; not bad about the situation PLUS isolated, avoidant, and touchy.

Much better version of bad, huh? From the standpoint of actionable guilt, you can more calmly examine the expectations of the patients themselves—and perfection, as mentioned, isn't one of them.

What *do* patients expect from us? It's actually pretty simple: to understand what they're going through, and to clearly explain our understanding—of both what happened, and what's going to happen next.

Beyond that, they want to know three things:

1. We're there for them.
2. We care about them.
3. We have—or aim to find—a solution for their problem.

None of those things can we give patients if we avoid them or approach the conversation coldly avoidant due to shame.

Paradoxically, when we're so into our heads about what people think about us, we can forget that we're here in service of others. We're here to help them. So, let's understand what they need help with.

When we clearly communicate what's happened and will happen, when patients know we're there for them, we care, and we're seeking solutions—that tells them we're worthy of trust.

Spiraling into avoidant shame can make us objectively untrustworthy. Especially if it leads us to avoid confronting patients and disclosing the full picture of what's going on. When we withdraw and get stuck in our heads, we're not worthy of trust because we're not seeing things clearly. We're not effectively looking for solutions; we're wallowing in shame and self-blame instead.

Whatever you do, make sure the patient and their family know you're in this together—same team. If you feel comfortable doing so, share your cell number and let them reach out with questions. Above all, show them you're in it for the long haul, doing whatever you can to solve the problem.

The point was never for us to be perfect or feel great about ourselves. Nor should we make a big show of feeling terrible and punishing ourselves. The point is always for the patient to feel better, and to give them hope. Ironically, when we own up to our mistakes and communicate completely, we also tend to feel better—and when we feel better, they do too.

INFORMED CONSENT

Part of why patients don't expect us to be perfect (aside from the fact that they know we're humans), is that we already told them things can go wrong. They literally signed a document stating that they're informed of the risks and limitations of medical treatment, and they consent to it anyway.

That's why patients sign a consent to treat every time they step into a doctor's office—and why lawyers and admins make such a big deal about it. Informed consent is not some rote, meaningless administrative formality to collect signatures then toss them aside. It's something physicians are directly responsible for, and we should approach it that way.

True informed consent should be an interactive process in which you, the physician, thoroughly explain what can go wrong. Remind patients that, by signing the informed consent, they confirm that they understand and accept these risks.

Especially when it comes to a high-risk procedure like an invasive operation, we must clearly explain the risks—potential infections, bleeding, intestinal leak, drug-drug interactions, etc.—before patients sign.

Some doctors would rather avoid bringing up potentially negative outcomes. They'd prefer to maintain a positive, hopeful front for patients at all times. The truth is, by adequately preparing your patients, you show them respect and set yourself up for trust.

Besides, if you've outlined common complications—and the fact that these things can happen regardless of a surgeon's skill level—patients will be less surprised should something go wrong. If you do face an angry or disgruntled patient, you can remind them of both your previous conversations and what the informed consent document means.

When patients are truly informed, they feel part of a team—and they're more likely to think, "This sucks, but she said it might happen," rather than, "My doctor screwed up."

The same goes for physicians, by the way. Instead of dismissing these possibilities as things that only happen to lesser doctors, let's embrace the fact that we are also consenting to all possible risks and outcomes—just like our patients.

REDEFINE "FAILURE"

Too often, we confuse complications with failures. Again, if they're caused by egregious, preventable errors, that's one thing. But as we know, complications can and will happen—eventually—regardless.

Instead, reframe complications as imperfect outcomes. Remind yourself that you're human. Not only that, but even your (hypothetical and impossible) perfection could not guarantee 100 percent optimal outcomes.

Clearly you should also do everything in your power to prevent complications on your watch. In the next chapter, we'll talk about how to track and analyze your own performance. But while you don't want a pattern of mishaps, perfectionism can also be a career killer.

In my mind, true failure comes not from messing up, but rather from not dealing with the mistake afterwards.

CULTIVATING SHAME RESILIENCE

It's time to disband the Itty Bitty Shitty Committee. Without severance. They've never done a thing for you. At the end of the day, you're allowed to be human—as long as you're consistently doing your best and taking accountability. Sure, if you made a mistake because you were up late drinking tequila the night before the surgery, that's different.

What Julia's facing occurs quite often. Her reaction demonstrates how the perfection trap self-directs blame—before we even confirm cause. Maybe there was a stitch off, but it's just as possible Julia did the procedure exactly right, and it just didn't take.

Shame is understandable. Complications come at true cost to the patient. Every surgeon faces the need to reoperate at some point in their career, but even though we know it's almost unavoidable, it's still awful.

Shame resilience doesn't mean we never feel bad. It simply means that we shift our feelings to actionable guilt. In other words, we define the situation—including, perhaps, our own actions—as regrettable, rather than defining *ourselves* as "bad."

"I'm bad" is a fixed state. There's nowhere to go from there, so we'll just carry the label around with us. Every time we make a mistake or see an imperfect outcome, we say, "See? There's proof!" Then we're far more likely to create that reality for ourselves by avoiding others, communicating ineffectively, and rejecting the support we need to resolve the issue.

Guilt provides direction. We can take accountability, apologize if needed, explain the situation, and work toward a solution.

FACE THE MUSIC

After talking a moment to regain composure, Julia realizes she has a choice. She can further damage the patient relationship by avoiding confrontation or showing up to the pre-op conversation guarded and distressed. Or, she can get over herself and go face this difficult patient conversation in a healthy way.

Julia chooses the latter. Once she explains to the patient what's going on, she's surprised to see he doesn't seem upset. In fact, his first response is, "Thanks for the clear explanation," followed by: "You said this might happen."

Following the (successful!) colostomy, Julia decides to suck it up and apologize to Robert for snapping at him earlier.

"I get it," he says in response. "I've been there myself."

We're all susceptible to assuming everybody else is doing a better—more perfect—job. Part of that is the perfection trap, and part of it is lack of data. How do we know what's normal? Are we seeing too many complications with our patients?

It's hard to answer this question because we don't meaningfully track complications at a large scale. Sure, we're "supposed to," and some resources exist, but not in a comprehensive way. The next chapter will explore why that is, and how we can instead measure and analyze performance by tracking our own data.

NEXT STEPS

1. Consider all complications that could arise for your next procedure and plan how to deal with each.
2. Pay attention to what you tell yourself after a complication. Compare that to what patients tell you—and to what you would tell a colleague in a similar situation.
3. How do you cope with complications—venting, obsessively researching, isolating? Do these behaviors serve you and your patients?

BOSS PODCAST EPISODES:

https://www.BOSSsurgery.com/podcasts/
boss-business-of-surgery-series

Ep. 2: *Why We Became Surgeons*

Ep. 21: *Shame Resilience and What Patients Really Want after Complications*

Ep. 10: *You Don't Have to Dread Call, with Dr. Karen Leitner*

CHAPTER 10

PERFORMANCE ANALYSIS

After his first surgery led to complications, Julia's patient did not conclude that she was a terrible doctor. Having listened when she explained risks, he understood that things could go wrong (including what actually did). Most importantly, he saw that Julia was there for him. She explained things clearly, showed that she cared, and resolved the problem.

The subsequent emergency colostomy was a success in more ways than one. Not only did the procedure go smoothly, but it also helped Julia understand how perfectionism tricked her into doubting her worth. She compared herself not only to her colleague Robert, but also to some imaginary flawless ideal.

Julia finds herself thinking back—almost fondly—to her weekly mortality and morbidity (M&M) conferences from residency. She never thought she'd actually *miss* the grim exercise of analyzing deaths and complications, but with everyone openly sharing, it seemed less scary and isolating. After residency, there's no equivalent practice for attending physicians to come together and discuss negative outcomes.

Julia realizes she needs a legitimate metric to assess her own performance. One more objective and accurate than uninformed assumptions about what everyone else *might* be doing. *How often do such complications actually happen?* she wonders. *There's got to be some kind of comprehensive database.*

She asks Robert if he knows any resources like that.

"Short answer? Not really," he says, adding: "There's something like that, but it's self-reported. How many doctors do you think voluntarily report to a national database when things go wrong?"

SELF-REPORTED DATA

Without comprehensive data, we're left with biases (often against ourselves) or impressions we have of what others might be doing. So how does Julia—or any physician—more accurately assess performance?

I posted the following questions in a couple social media groups of fellow surgeons: "Do you track personal outcomes for complications? Do you know of national or regional databases that track complication rates?"

Crickets.

To be fair, a few national databases do track medical outcomes, such as the Surveillance, Epidemiology, and End Results (SEER) program by the National Cancer Institute, and the National Surgical Quality Improvement Program (NSQIP) through the American College of Surgeons. In fact, NSQIP's motto is: "To improve quality, first measure quality."

However, these and other efforts focus on improving quality at the *hospital* level. They do not track individual physician data. While it may be possible to formally request a breakdown of your own personal physician outcomes, it would prove cumbersome and time-consuming to tease out that information. (SEER requires an official research proposal for such requests.) Plus, you'd have to request this information monthly or quarterly, adding another administrative layer to your (and others') work.

Someone eventually posted a response about a wound infection database maintained by their hospital—but again it's self-reported, and most surgeons decline to participate in such programs. Including myself, actually. I recall getting letters from a former employer about voluntarily tracking complications related to surgical site infections. I participated twice. The first time because I thought that I had to. The second time I thought maybe I should. After that, I thought, *Why would I track this if there's even a remote chance it could be used to hurt me?*

Whether it's a personality quiz or a wound infection database, the basic tenet of self-reported data holds true: Crap in = crap out.

Complications generate fears about our reputations and compensation. Especially when we falsely equate imperfect outcomes with failure, sending even an anonymous report can *feel* like risking exposure.

Besides, who has the time? With so much else going on, the only reason many of us even know how many cases we have is through billing.

We may want to know if our complications are higher than average, but until we develop enough collective shame resilience to at least approach a 100 percent participation rate of honestly shared data, we can only accurately evaluate our own isolated, personal trends.

The onus is on us to figure out our own personal success and complication rates, and improve those. This chapter discusses how to track personal outcomes and more objectively analyze performance trends as individual physicians.

PERFORMANCE TRENDS

Professional athletes analyze their stats each week—for good reason. The data helps them assess and improve performance. Likewise, as a physician, developing clear metrics can help you gauge both your individual progress and the validity of outside feedback.

Unlike the NFL, we don't have statisticians tracking our every move in the field. Nor do we typically hold weekly physician huddles to crunch numbers on team performance. This likely results from our culture of individualism, plus avoidance rooted in perfection. When so many of us default to an avoidant shame response as individuals, it makes sense that there's generalized shame around imperfect outcomes at the collective level too. Sure, you can read an article or two and get a rough sense of what medical analysts think about complication rates, but these don't tend to be super accessible or comprehensive.

While variations in patient populations impact the helpfulness of these databases, their main flaw is underreporting. No one wants to talk about their negative outcomes. When we do, we unconsciously (or consciously) try to present ourselves in a better light—especially when it affects our livelihoods.

It may be hard to meaningfully compare yourself to others, but that doesn't matter as much as you might think. After all, you have little to no control over how others perform. What you can control is your own personal performance trends. You don't actually have to be "better" than the next physician, but you should progress.

TELL YOURSELF THE TRUTH

Many of us procrastinate on tracking our performance data, or we struggle to keep it up. There's probably a reason for that. Maybe you've had experiences in the past where you admitted fault and felt punished or shamed.

How can you create safety around this? Start by keeping your performance data to yourself—and by being kind to yourself.

If you hear a strange noise at night, hiding under the bed won't make you feel safer. Similarly, tucking your complication rates under the rug won't make you a better surgeon. So how do you get better?

By gathering accurate information. As discussed in Chapter 1, there's so much power in honest self-examination—especially when the truth feels uncomfortable. This goes back to personal responsibility.

You don't have to share your personal performance tracking with anyone. The only person truly worthy of competition is *you yesterday*. That's not to say you can't have a bad day here and there. If you're honest, you will see dips in self-reported performance along the way. But as long as your general performance consistently trends upward, that's success.

We avoid self-examination because we're afraid of what we'll find and what it's going to mean. But at what cost? Complication rates and other performance factors remain whether we track them or not. If we refuse to look, we deny ourselves growth and improvement. How can we improve if we don't know our baseline? How can we track progress with no data or metrics?

We're so afraid this information will be used to punish us that we lose track of the point, which is to get better. By recognizing the fear, we can begin to neutralize it and instead focus on progress.

START TRACKING

Analyzing your performance doesn't have to be cumbersome or time-consuming. It can be as simple as creating a spreadsheet, then sitting down once a week—or even once a month—to plug in whatever numbers you'd like to track. How did this week go in terms of wound infections or other complications? How did this month go?

If you're not sure how performance tracking translates to your specialty, keep it general: "How do I feel about my performance this week?" Create an arbitrary scoring system: "On a scale of zero to ten, I performed at an eight."

It may seem vague, but there's value in jotting down how you feel each day for later review. It keeps you from exaggerating the importance of how you feel on any given day. When people mess up or get triggered, they often tell themselves they're "always" messing up or feeling this way. Try jotting down for a month how you're doing each day—scale of zero to ten. The results may surprise you.

Without measurement, it's easier to exaggerate and catastrophize negative experiences. This happens with both surgical outcomes and book writing. On days when I feel unmotivated, avoidant, or foggy-headed, it feels like I'll "never" get this book done. However, if I'd been tracking how I feel each day about this project, I could probably reassure myself that bad days don't last forever.

Speaking of books, President Joe Biden wrote about this very thing in his memoir *Promise Me, Dad*, about grieving his son Beau's death. His therapist advised that he apply a number to how he felt each day. While it seemed arbitrary at first, after a while he began to understand his baseline and patterns. On those "zero" days of despair—when the pain seemed to swallow him up—he could see that, in the past, he'd always pulled back up…a little at a time.

Everyone, from physicians to presidents, endures loss. It's helpful to take daily emotional inventory, but sometimes—like when we inevitably lose a patient—those feelings can overwhelm. When this happens, we need to process what comes up. One idea is to light a small candle each night. Then, simply pause and reflect on the patient and everything the situation brings up. Each night, as the candle burns down, allow yourself to also release and accept. Small rituals like this can help honor the experience—to both process feelings and let them go.

Grief is a slow, winding process. One day feels like sheer hell, and the next day, only minimally less terrible. While we all overestimate how quickly we're "supposed to" (or would like to) recover, we can easily underestimate just how much healing we've done and how much progress we've made.

EXTERNAL FEEDBACK

This applies beyond our self-observed outcomes to external feedback as well. If you don't track performance metrics, you're at the mercy of external feedback. If you happen to be in a supportive environment with honest, yet kind and judicious, colleagues, that may be okay. Otherwise, it could be a big problem. Either way, without independent self-assessment, it's harder to objectively evaluate the validity of others' feedback— whether from colleagues, administrators, or patients.

Humans harbor a negativity bias, especially for outside feedback. We're far more likely to disproportionately weigh negative information, which our bodies register as a potential threat.

When we don't track and measure our own performance, we outsource our evaluation to others—not to mention our self-worth. This can result in endlessly chasing compliments to compensate for disproportionately weighted negative interactions. Until we internalize self-worth, we'll crave ever-higher volumes of complimentary feedback (think chasing "likes" on social media), just to feel okay.

No amount of external validation and praise will suffice if we're too scared to evaluate our own growth. But whether through self-reported performance data or external feedback, we don't have to interpret imperfect outcomes as threats. Instead, let's reframe both constructive criticism and imperfect outcomes as helpful, desirable data. By examining mistakes, we learn how not to repeat them.

While obviously trying our best to avoid negative outcomes, let's accept that crap happens, then seek data about it—on purpose. That's how we become better physicians and better human beings.

CHANGE YOUR PATTERNS

Once you start examining mistakes and complications, you'll learn a lot about how you process them. What happens when you do something regrettable? Does part of you minimize, justify, blame-shift, or retreat? Do you resort to black-or-white thinking, then beat yourself up?

Start honestly, if privately, tracking complications, and you'll begin to accept imperfect outcomes as not only part of the process, but also as valuable opportunities to learn about yourself and reset your course.

The answer to uncertainty and perfectionism is information and data.

As Brené Brown puts it, "Shame does not survive the light of day." So when faced with regrettable outcomes, cast light on your own shame. Believe it or not, it helps to consciously plan in advance how we want to feel about negative outcomes. Literally just decide. Tell yourself: "I want to feel curious about my mistakes, patient with myself, and motivated to course-correct and improve."

That doesn't mean you'll immediately, magically succeed in "achieving" this response. Eisenhower said, "No plan survives contact with the enemy. It's the ability to adapt that leads to good leaders." He also said, "Plans are useless. But planning is indispensable."

Plan ahead of time, but don't get too attached to the plan. Recognize that, while your plan may not survive contact with a real-life complication, the act of planning helps. Just thinking about this stuff can help you have a more robust conversation about risk and achieve more informed consent with patients.

Extend this logic to how you respond to criticism. Decide in advance how you'd like to weigh external feedback. Be realistic, of course. It may never feel great to hear criticism—but you can decide to not let it ruin your day, your self-esteem, or your career.

AIM FOR IMPROVEMENT, NOT PERFECTION

Creating a personal data tracking system is a great first step to analyzing and improving performance at work—and maybe it stops there. Or you may want to share this powerful tool with your team, especially if you're in a leadership role.

At the very least, committing to a personal practice of self-evaluation can make you more patient and supportive of colleagues. It certainly helps you to avoid unnecessarily comparing yourself to others.

It also helps you realize that life is a bell curve between abject failure and misery on one side, and pure success and ecstasy on the other—with a whole lot of bulk in between. If you track outcomes and feelings, you'll find pretty quickly that neither constant perfection nor 24/7 happiness are reasonable goals. Meanwhile, you're likely not doing as bad as you thought.

Remind yourself why you entered medicine in the first place. Probably, your answer is something like "To help people." You certainly wouldn't say: "To show the world how impressively perfect I am!"

Likewise, the purpose of tracking outcomes is to help—both others, and yourself. Not to become perfect, but to consistently progress. After all, that's the whole point of M&M conferences: to create a habit of reflection, self-assessment, and consistent improvement.

Once Julia begins tracking both her personal complication rates and her daily outlook, she sees how different aspects of work impact how she *feels* about her daily performance. One sticking point is clinical notes, which still seem to pile up no matter what she does.

Julia's not alone. Many physicians get into a cycle of resentment and avoidance with unfinished clinical notes. However, far from some tedious chore, clinical notes represent essential communications—and an important resource for self-examination.

Clinical notes provide archives of our patients' assessments, continuity of care, and all interactions, procedures, and results. In the next chapter, we'll discuss how to utilize this essential tool without letting it consume your mental bandwidth or your free time.

NEXT STEPS

1. Explore what metrics you can track (clinical visit/case volume, complication rates) to help you understand and improve personal outcomes.
2. Consider asking colleagues to weigh in on your clinical and financial outcomes. How does it feel to think about asking for feedback? What limiting thoughts hold you back?

RESOURCES:

National Surgery Quality Improvement Program: https://research.med.psu.edu/departments/surgery/nsqip-surgical-quality-improvement/#:~:text=The%20American%20College%20of%20Surgeons,the%20quality%20of%20surgical%20care

ACS Surgeon Specific Registry: https://www.facs.org/quality-programs/data-and-registries/surgeon-specific-registry/

CHAPTER 11

CLINICAL NOTES

Since tracking her performance data, Julia realizes that overall, her complication rates are decreasing. Plus, she has a clearer sense of how she's feeling from one day to the next. One (unsurprising) correlation stands out: on days when she's feeling more flustered, she's much more likely to bring home a pile of unfinished clinical notes.

This seems to be happening more. Maybe because, in trying to be more conscientious about performance assessment, Julia feels the need to take more thorough notes.

There never seems to be enough time to finish notes between patients, so Julia compensates by overdoing them at home. This cuts into her free time, leaving her exhausted and perpetuating a vicious cycle of resentment and procrastination.

FROM TASK TO TOOL

We've all been there. Staring at a stack of unfinished clinical notes, thinking: *The paperwork never ends. This is why I'm so burned out!*

That's not getting to the heart of the issue. When we feel burned out, we overestimate workloads. Stacks of clinical notes provide an easy symbol of overwhelm when we're looking for something to blame. *These notes take too long; electronic medical records are tedious; they keep adding patients to my clinic; etc.*

There may be truth to these statements, but let's get realistic about how long things like clinical notes actually need to take. To thrive as a physician and maintain sanity, efficiency is key. If you're feeling overwhelmed, look at what you can modify. Where can you shave off unnecessary time?

When clinical notes feel overwhelming, the natural tendency is to put them off. This makes matters worse. Rehearsing a story about "all this stuff I have to do" disempowers you.

Take a moment to consider the purpose and value of clinical notes. How could you do your job without an archive of information about each patients' care history? Rather than viewing this as some burdensome task you *have to do*, reframe it as an invaluable tool you *get to employ*—to make things better for yourself, your colleagues, and your patients.

In other words, try practicing this mindset shift: From "I *have* to do this" to "I *get* to do this—to share knowledge and provide a record for both the patient and their medical team to know what's happening to them."

Clinical notes are not exactly a treat. Though it may sound

simple, it's never an *easy* shift from straight up dread to some enlightened state of appreciation and focused execution.

Let's start out with something easier. Take a moment to assess how you feel *before* doing notes. Do you feel resentful or overwhelmed before even starting? Recognizing the emotion you feel beforehand can tell you a lot about the issue and how to reframe your outlook.

Next, decide how you *want* to feel about notes. Remind yourself of their value, and give yourself a plan for getting from point A (how you feel now) to point B (how you want to feel).

This chapter offers concrete tips to reframe your outlook on clinical notes and more efficiently employ this essential tool moving forward. The first step? Simplify your approach.

PARE IT DOWN

Compared to my early-career standards, I've lately written some pretty crappy notes—and I'm perfectly okay with that. Though to be fair, the description of "crappy" only holds true if I'm holding my notes to college thesis standards.

When I first started, I fell right into the perfectionism trap with clinical notes. Erring on the side of over-communication, I typed out complete sentences comprising full paragraphs, diligently edited for spelling or punctuation errors. Talk about diminishing returns!

When trapped in a burnout cycle, we tend to defend overwork. Part of this is perfectionism, but it also has to do with the sunk cost fallacy. We're more likely to double down on a way of doing something if we've already invested a lot of time or other resources into it. But when we persist in overdoing clinical notes, we don't redeem our past overwork; we just burn ourselves out more.

We also make things harder for everyone else. Let's get one thing straight: No one—not one person—wants to read your long-winded block of text. No one cares about your typos or grammatical mistakes. Clinical notes are not story time, and they're not a graded assignment for English composition.

Keep notes short and sweet. To do their job, clinical notes need only convey the most basic clinical information. Your notes should read as a clear, concise outline of essential data only.

FORCED URGENCY

When we forget the value of clinical notes, it's easy to disregard them as "busy work" to put off. It's time to reframe them as a key asset for your entire team, and a core aspect of your work in clinic—without overdoing them.

You have two choices: You can either fully incorporate notes into your workflow, or you can pile them for later. Many young physicians take the latter approach. It's easy to put off paperwork, but all this does is create more work overall—and more resentment.

Instead, employ what I call "forced urgency." When it's time for clinical notes, focus and execute, immediately. When tackling any perceived chore or interruption with forced urgency, something amazing happens: *It actually gets done.* Efficiently, in real time. Then, with the task complete, it goes away—poof!—instead of following you home.

In other words, notes aren't distractions from your work. They *are* the work. If you want to get the most out of clinical notes without the headaches, they need to be done—now.

Yes, *now.*

KEEP IT IN CLINIC

By "now," I mean in the clinic itself. Once you master minimalism in clinical notes, you can easily keep this task where it belongs.

The physician's life is extremely action-oriented. We zoom from one task to the next—*doing, doing, doing.* I believe this is why we dread clinical notes. Because they require us to pause the busyness and formulate thoughts.

Where do we have time for this kind of work? In the clinic. For me, staying on top of clinical notes got a whole lot easier when I vowed to complete all notes while physically with the patient.

At first, something in me resisted. It told me I needed to give my patients undivided attention—that I couldn't possibly listen attentively and build rapport while typing notes. *I'll remember later*, I'd think. But after seeing twenty patients in a row, I don't remember much. No one does.

When I began completing notes in clinic, I was surprised by

how little it impacted my ability to pay attention or build and maintain relationships. Patients truly don't mind. If you're still worried about it, speak to that. Let the patient know you'll be typing as you speak, because you value the information they give you and want them to have the best possible care.

Let's reevaluate what's going on during clinic. Early in my career, I recall reading a study suggesting that physicians usually identify a patient's problem in about thirty seconds. While I wasn't able to locate that exact publication, it's generally understood that, most of the time, we figure things out pretty quickly. Obviously our patient visits last longer than thirty seconds though—for good reason.

Say Julia's patient needs their gallbladder taken out. During a clinical encounter, she may review their ultrasound, confirm their history, make sure they're not on blood thinners, and check for universal complications. Along the way comes rapport-building banter, as the patient cracks jokes or chats about their new hairdresser or neighbor's dog.

In short, there's more "down time" built into clinical encounters than Julia might realize. Once she stops being precious or perfectionistic about notes, she realizes she can easily converse with patients and jot down all necessary information. It's up to every one of us, as physicians, to build and maintain rapport while keeping ourselves on track—and being able to type as we talk and listen is part of that.

We also need support. Nurses and support staff can help, both with taking notes before we enter the room and with building in time between patients so we can complete unfinished notes. When you share this work, it lightens your plate while empowering colleagues to get involved in info-gathering and relationship-building with patients. As attendings, it's up to us to build this collaboration through skillful delegation.

Like clinical note taking, delegation feels time-consuming and inefficient. "It's easier to just do it myself" is a common myth—not to mention a self-fulfilling prophecy. If you never bother training your team, you'll never get adequate support.

Done right, delegation builds collaboration and efficiency among your team and helps everyone buy into the mission of better serving patients. But delegation is a skill most of us never properly learned. The next chapter explores how to ask for and receive help in a way that actually saves time and empowers everyone involved.

NEXT STEPS
1. Evaluate your feelings and beliefs about clinical notes.
2. Identify where you can streamline notes or visit interactions to keep notes in clinic.

BOSS PODCAST EPISODES:

https://www.BOSSsurgery.com/podcasts/
boss-business-of-surgery-series

Ep. 35: *Improving Clinic Efficiency, with Dr. Sarah Beth Snell*

Ep. 49: *Stop Hating Clinic*

Ep. 69: *Mid-Career Slump and a Better Use of Clinic Time, with Dr. David Canes*

Ep. 55: *Working with an NP/PA, with Dr. Seaworth*

CHAPTER 12

DELEGATION

Tired of scrambling through clinic, Julia decides to tighten her note taking and revisit her clinical schedule. Rather than feeling directed by the workflow around her, she realizes she can flip the script and direct the workflow instead.

Julia stays up late outlining exactly how she'd like her clinical scheduling to change, plus ways her nurses can better support other administrative tasks. The next morning, she passes out instructions to both the office staff and her nurses. She also emails related spreadsheets, cc'ing her partners.

This afternoon, however, she finds her nurse, Claire, in the clinic scrolling through her phone. When Julia asks about the new schedule draft, it wasn't done.

We talked about this! Julia thinks. *I made a detailed list explaining exactly what to do and how to do it.*

Julia feels frustrated and helpless. She tried so hard to clarify what she wants from those around her—and they're still dropping the ball. Julia's suspected for a while that Claire isn't fond of her, especially considering the facial expressions—and that *tone*—she seems to reserve just for Julia. This apparent defiance seems to confirm everything.

WHY DO WE DELEGATE?

Before launching into where and how Julia's attempt to delegate went wrong, let's ask: Why do we delegate? The simple answer is to maximize our limited resources of time and effort.

How? By better coordinating among team members. After all, if you have to do everything yourself, you'll never consistently improve outcomes—let alone scale efforts.

To achieve this, we must delegate *skillfully*. Otherwise, we risk exacerbating bottlenecks of time and effort, or even creating new bottlenecks ourselves.

As medical students and residents, we didn't get much practice directing support staff. Instead, we try to excel by doing too much. It's important to remember that, as clinical leaders within our teams, we are 100 percent responsible for the outcomes we get, but that doesn't mean we have to *do* it all.

This chapter explores three main elements of delegation: (1) Reframing the work, (2) Nurturing both mastery and recognition, and (3) Understanding the appropriate level of delegation needed for each unique situation and person.

When approached with these elements in mind, delegation

empowers everyone to synchronize and optimize efforts, making the best use of time and other limited resources.

REFRAME "INTERRUPTIONS"

Whether we like it or not, as attendings, we must collaborate with admin to train and mentor both support staff and younger colleagues. These team members inevitably interrupt our workflow with questions. They need our expertise, guidance, and attention to do their jobs—and help us do ours.

Remember the lesson of "forced urgency?" As with clinical notes, it's easy to view delegation as interruptions, rather than an integral part of the work itself. But by stopping to immediately direct, correct, or advise, we end up saving a lot of time in the end.

Consciously integrate delegation into your workflow. Then, expect interruptions and decide ahead of time how you want to react (I recommend focus and patience).

Finally, employ forced urgency. If a colleague or support staff comes to you with a question, stop what you're doing. For one moment, make this the most important thing. Focus entirely on the matter, resolve it, and carry on. If you've communicated clearly and delegated skillfully—congratulations!—you've just invested in more efficient collaboration down the line.

MASTERY AND RECOGNITION

When it comes to delegation, things can go very wrong—quickly. However, what may feel like an interpersonal relationship problem may actually be about something completely different.

As discussed in Chapters 6 (Relationship Dynamics) and 7 (Group Dynamics), we oversimplify and distort when we assign victim and villain roles. These labels almost never apply to what's really going on. Not only do they project our own insecurities, they also create or reinforce divisions.

Effective delegation involves mastery and recognition. Everyone works best when they feel growing mastery over their jobs and others acknowledge their efforts and progress.

Sometimes delegation fails to build mastery because we assume people know more than they do. Overwhelmed with tasks, we may dump them on another's plate with inadequate instruction. If we overestimate their capacity or expertise, we transfer our overwhelm to them. Now, instead of someone lifting you out of the muck, you've dragged them down with you.

We can also err in the direction of overly detailed delegating. When we do this, we undermine mastery and recognition by removing freedom. We overestimate the value of *our* perspective while undervaluing that of those around us. This feels disrespectful, overbearing, or even downright insulting.

The second approach is often termed micromanagement—and it's exactly what Julia did with her team. By abruptly redirecting every aspect of her nurse's administrative workflow, Julia prevents her from becoming a master at her own work. In an effort to avoid her own burnout, Julia imposed rigid, overly detailed instructions that failed to recognize Claire's skills or experience—or even her agency at all. In effect, Julia robbed Claire of both mastery and recognition.

When it came to the new schedule draft, Julia also left out one key piece of information that Claire actually needed: when the task was supposed to be completed. Without an agreed upon deadline, the gap between assigning a task and seeing it completed can devolve into a void of insecurity, overwhelm, and frustration.

FIVE LEVELS OF DELEGATION

In his book, *Your World Class Assistant*, Michael Hyatt discusses how best to hire and train an executive assistant—including great insight into effective delegation. He describes five different levels:

- Level 1: Do exactly what I tell you. Report back frequently and do not deviate.
- Level 2: Research the issue and report back with options. We'll discuss, then I'll decide what to do.
- Level 3: Research the issue, outline options, and make your recommendation. I'll consider and approve your recommendation (or not).
- Level 4: Make a decision and tell me what you did. I trust you did the research and made the best decision. Just keep me in the loop so I'm not surprised.
- Level 5: Do what you think is best; no need to report back. I trust you completely. You have my full support.

Problems arise when we apply the wrong level to an individual or situation. If I told a new administrative assistant: "Alphabetize these files in that cabinet," that's pretty clear. If I just said, "Organize all my files," that could be interpreted in different ways—some helpful, others less so.

Now if I said, "Alphabetize these files and in folders color-coded by diagnosis, with label tabs arranged in a zig-zag pattern—while sitting in this chair, facing 130 degrees southeast at high noon," that would obviously be overkill.

It's on you to figure out which level is appropriate—though you may have guessed that levels one and five are rarely applicable. While level one allows no room for collaboration or innovation, level five requires mind reading, which leads to mistakes and resentment.

Let's return to Julia's crowded clinical schedule. If, like hers, your clinic keeps getting overbooked, one option is to go to your nurse and simply say, "I'm overbooked. Please look at my schedule and fix it."

This lets the other person decide what "overbooked" looks like. If they're not sure what you want, they're more likely to procrastinate—or do it incorrectly, then suffer the consequences.

Especially with a new or inexperienced person, explain what an appropriate schedule looks like to you. For example: "Please give me twenty minutes between patients to finish my notes."

If you're dealing with someone who's been around for years, explain the issue and ask for suggestions. Experienced support staff often see aspects of the situation you don't. If you show zero faith in their perspective, you disempower them, while depriving yourself of valuable insights.

When delegating at a level four or five, it's still good to touch base. Even seasoned professionals have doubts, so don't leave room for mind-reading. Check in from time to time to fill gaps and reinforce where they're doing well.

When you over-delegate, as Julia did, you trap everybody in one rigid way of doing things (*your* way). You're less receptive to recommendations or innovation, and you haven't empowered anyone to collaborate, only to await orders.

Sometimes, a single relationship goes through different levels, starting with mostly levels one or two and evolving to a more hands-off approach. It depends on the task at hand and each individual's experience, expertise, and work style. Some people naturally crave detailed directions. Others do better with a hands-off management style.

Hitting that balance takes trial and error. You'll need grace on both sides, as well as proper communication. When we leave a vacuum of information, others fill it with their own assumptions (or insecurities).

DELEGATE YOUR THOUGHT PROCESS

Proper communication means explaining your thought process for *why* this needs done and *how* to get there. It helps to walk them through a task the first time, answering questions along the way.

When we make people read our minds, we may later assume they're doing it "wrong" out of incompetence or disrespect. Ultimately, we didn't recognize their thought process, which may be simply: "I don't yet fully understand X."

When I hired my nurse practitioner (NP), I had her spend a

week with me in the inpatient setting, just following me around, watching and listening as I narrated key parts of what I was doing and why. I also shared my own experiences with uncertainty, overwhelm, and personal error—and how I dealt with these. Basically, I paid her full hourly fee to observe, ask questions, and do little else. Not only did this allow me to delegate my thought process, it also paid back interest when it came to avoiding mistakes and time-consuming discussions down the line.

When explaining thought processes, focus on outcomes. What's the ultimate goal? *Why* are you doing this?

I often give coaching clients the following exercise: Make a list of complaints—say, regarding clinic. In column a, write down everything you hate about clinic. In column b, write down what you'd rather have instead. Finally, in column c, write down the underlying reason—what's the great desire driving all this?

This exercise challenges you to figure out both *how* to solve a problem, and also *why* it needs solved. We tend to focus a lot on the *how*, but that's not always the main point. Often the *why* is non-negotiable, while the *how* remains flexible.

If our goals include maximizing time and effort, empowering those around us, and best serving patients, *how* we achieve them can stay fluid. By keeping the focus on the *why*, we invite new strategies and perspectives for achieving goals. Suddenly, the problem refocuses, changing from some overwhelming, amorphous threat to a clear list of both objectives to overcome and potential solutions.

CURIOSITY, EMPOWERMENT, AND APPRECIATION

Check how you feel when trying to get help. Maybe you're afraid this person doesn't like you, that they're not good at their job, or even that they're trying to somehow sabotage you.

Maybe you're right. Then again, maybe something else is going on. Try channeling a more helpful emotion—one that empowers you both. When delegating, I aim to approach in the spirit of curiosity, empowerment, and appreciation.

Getting curious means asking questions and actually listening: *What specifically went wrong? What tools or resources do you need to get the job done? What feedback do you have for me about how I directed you?* By gathering info, you can assess what's going on and come to a more collaborative solution.

Empowerment sounds like, "I know you can do this. We just have to find the right way forward." Such statements soothe defensiveness, allay potential misinterpretations, and build confidence. When you occupy a position of authority, you influence not only how people around you feel about *you*, but also about how they feel about themselves—and that reflects in how they treat you in turn.

Finally, find reasons to show appreciation, even when outcomes aren't ideal. You could say, "I see how hard you're working on this," before together exploring where things got off track. Maybe the only thing you can appreciate is the fact that they're exhausted and overwhelmed at this moment. (If you're reading this book, I'm guessing you know how that feels.)

Changing my own script to reflect curiosity, empowerment, and appreciation yields far better outcomes than knee-jerk suspicion, annoyance, or resentment. That said, it's hard to break old habits, and sometimes "fake it til you make it" backfires. I once worked with a surgeon who told me: "I don't know why people are so touchy around me. I mean, I think they're all idiots, but it's not like I *tell them* that."

Trust me, they can tell.

It's especially tricky when there's an ingrained pattern of mistrust with a coworker, and they regularly approach you with projections and negative emotions. In this situation, remind yourself that, as the attending physician (or any position of leadership), you remain 100 percent responsible for your team's outcomes.

Take a deep breath and focus on the goal. Practice reframing your emotions and stories before interacting with others. In the case of my former colleague, he might start with: "I think they're all idiots...but I could be missing something."

You cannot control every outcome, but you can choose—little by little, day by day—to get *curious*, *empower* those around you, and better *appreciate* both other people's efforts and their points of view.

Positive, constructive emotions cultivate trust and respect. Rather than dividing everyone into roles of victim or villain, seek to reconcile and unite. Then—together—you can figure out what's going on and where to go from there.

ASSESS AND REDIRECT

What kind of a manager are you? Do you fall into the trap of over-delegating, or do you assume everyone should already know what you want?

It's normal to miscalculate. If you're new to directing others, start small. Outsource just one or two tasks from your plate at a time. This helps you figure out your own patterns and pitfalls, and gather outside feedback—both about how you can better direct, and about the strengths and challenges of your teammates.

Redirect focus to three main outcomes: (1) Cultivating a sense of mastery and recognition among your entire team, (2) Communicating the *why*, while allowing flexibility in *how* you get there, and (3) Keeping everyone on the same page.

When my coaching clients do the three-columns exercise, the number one *why* behind what they hate about clinic tends to be: "I want my time and effort to be valued."

We can get mad at all the tiny things people do to "make us feel" like our time or effort is wasted…or we can simply communicate this bigger picture concern. Chances are, this goal is shared by everyone around us.

Finally, to collaboratively find the best way forward, approach issues with curiosity, empowerment, and appreciation.

If Julia communicated with her nurse in this way, she would realize Claire didn't know *when* Julia wanted a new schedule of the draft. She may also discover that Claire had ideas about how to resolve the scheduling issue, but she didn't feel Julia was receptive to her point of view. Because Claire felt both under-appreciated and overwhelmed by her own perfection trap, she avoided the task altogether.

This part of the book, on improving outcomes—indeed, most of the book so far—has focused mainly on interpersonal dynamics and career fulfillment. Success also involves understanding larger structures and limitations in our medical system, including the money cycle that governs how we get paid.

Part 4 takes a closer look at systems of coding, billing and reimbursement, insurance, and clinical finances. While this may sound tedious or technical, the purpose of this section is not to bog you down with dreary calculations or dense jargon. Instead, the goal is to better understand *why* these systems are in place, and—most importantly—how to get them to work in your favor.

NEXT STEPS

1. Note which essential tasks you consider interruptions, and employ forceful urgency to complete these with less mental drama.
2. Explain delegation levels to your team. Communicate which level you're using for each task and why.
3. Delegate your thought process. Demonstrate how you do the task, explaining how and why. Next, watch them do the task, seeking to understand their thought process.

PART 4

FOLLOW
THE MONEY

CHAPTER 13

CRACKING THE CODING

On her way to a department head one-on-one, Julia feels optimistic and confident. She knows she's been doing great work—after all, she's been tracking outcomes and dialing in both clinical notes and delegation. Imagine her surprise when she hears she won't be getting her expected bonus.

"My contract includes a production-based bonus," she objects. "I've been working hard and getting good results."

"You have," he responds. "We definitely see and appreciate your efforts. Unfortunately, your production bonus is not really about hours worked, or even outcomes, so much as work relative value units."

Ugh, Julia thinks. *Like I don't have enough to keep track of without coding and billing nonsense. I swear they make things confusing just to pay us less.*

As Julia walks away, she's struck not only by the resentment she feels, but also by the nagging sense that, for all her high-level expertise and skill, she understands little about an essential part of her job: how she gets paid. Rather than indulging in bitterness and self-pity, Julia decides it's time to learn more about the money cycle.

SOLVE AND SHOW YOUR WORK

We all want to get paid what we're worth. It seems like that should be easy. If we can transplant organs, create bionic prosthetics, and overcome deadly diseases with vaccines, can't we also develop a clear, simple, and fair physician reimbursement system?

The truth is that while the money cycle may seem unnecessarily complicated, it actually does follow comprehensible and predictable rules. As a resident, your flat-fee pay wasn't directly related to these rules, since you weren't paid by how you determined diagnoses, ordered procedures, or prescribed medicine.

Meanwhile, the money cycle isn't taught in residency—a fact I find both surprising and unfortunate, since understanding can ensure full compensation and prevent mistakes or even fraud charges. Since we're not taught the rules, we often figure them out when we mess them up and someone tells us we're doing it wrong.

This sparks mental drama, entrenching our victim mentality. When mishaps occur, we have the option of assuming the worst: *The system's messed up. I don't have time to keep track of it all. This is why I'm so burned out.*

Or, we can empower ourselves like the BOSS MDs we are, by learning how it all works.

Think of it this way: In school, you took on complicated (sometimes boring, technical, or seemingly irrelevant) material. Accelerated math and science courses prepared you for the complex, interconnected body systems you later mastered.

Here you are: a doctor! But guess what? You still have complex, technical systems to learn. Not just new medical procedures or discoveries, but also in terms of administrative complexities. Coding, as well as the process of billing and reimbursement through payer contracts—just like that required college chemistry course—might seem boring or difficult. But you've trained yourself to master complex systems (even boring, difficult ones).

Do yourself a favor and apply that same drive. Since the biggest problem lies in not understanding the rules, this chapter (and the next) will explore how coding works, and why. We'll also unpack billing and reimbursement through payer contracts, and how our paychecks fit into a broader system of clinical finances.

If you're thinking, *Yuck*, I get it. Don't worry; this isn't some dry textbook or glossary of terms. Without going into gritty detail, my goal is to provide a big picture overview so you can understand the broad mechanics and guiding principles of how money flows through the system and why.

Full disclosure, I am a surgeon, and this book reflects what I have been able to figure out on my own, within my field. While the devil's in the details, I've kept this section deliberately vague and general. It's up to you to fill in the details related to your work. Specific dollar amounts I use in examples are made up to clearly illustrate concepts. With anything this important, precise, and subject to change, check—and recheck—details related to your coding and reimbursement.

MONEY CYCLE

The relatively dull—but admittedly consequential—story of the money cycle begins with coding. Put simply, coding is a way to standardize, appraise, and compensate for the work we do.

As physicians, we provide services, both in the outpatient setting—which involves one set of codes—and in the inpatient setting—which involves another set of codes. Of course, there are modifiers, bundling, and exclusivity factors. Certain codes get bundled together while others don't. Some codes span a "global" period, encompassing a fixed or variable set of visits.

In short, it's complicated. But, as doctors, we can handle it.

Think of it as a math problem. A patient comes in with a problem. As doctors, we diagnose. Then, we solve and show our work. First, our diagnosis gets assigned an International Classification of Diseases (ICD-10) code.

Next, we assess what to do about the problem. This gets assigned an Evaluation and Management (E&M) code.

Finally, we carry out procedures, which get assigned a Current Procedural Terminology (CPT) code.

In short: Figure out the problem (ICD-10), evaluate the required level of care (E&M), then do something about it (CPT).

After that, someone at the medical practice creates an invoice to match ICD-10 codes with appropriate E&M and/or CPT codes. They submit this invoice for payment (billing), address any complaints (denials), and follow up to make sure both practice and practitioners get paid (collections).

On receiving invoices, payers assign facility relative value units (fRVUs) and work relative value units (wRVUs) to our E&M and CPT codes. Both kinds of RVUs measure how much our work is worth, as determined annually by the federal government's Centers for Medicare & Medicaid Services (CMS).

Based on their location, budget, and insurance payer mix, hospitals and medical practices next translate these units into payment for their medical facilities and payment for us, the providers.

I know—it's a lot already. For this chapter, we'll stick to the basics of the following medical codes: ICD-10, E&M, and CPT, along with common issues related to each. Then, Chapters 14 ("Getting Paid") and 15 ("Reimbursement Pitfalls") will unpack how we get paid, demystifying RVU codes and matters related to insurance billing and reimbursement.

DIAGNOSTICS

The ICD-10 diagnostic codes are determined and maintained by the United Nations' World Health Organization. Basically, a WHO committee decides to file heart failure under this code and gallstones under that one. This system standardizes the reporting of health patterns to help medical researchers monitor and analyze epidemiological population patterns. In other words, ICD-10 coding tracks the world's health data and supports the science of medicine by ensuring we all speak the same language.

Gallstones, and all diagnoses, have their own unique alpha-numeric code. So if you put "gallstones" in your clinical notes, most electronic medical records automatically suggest the correct coding.

In 2019, the WHO issued an update, the ICD-11, but this new set hasn't yet been widely adopted. In fact, as I write this, the US has barely adjusted to the ICD-10, which was mandated for all parties covered by the Health Insurance Portability and Accountability Act (HIPAA), not just providers who bill Medicare or Medicaid. When we all updated from ICD-9 to ICD-10, the many new details and changes frustrated doctors, coders, and insurance companies alike. In part because adding tens of thousands of new codes required massive (expensive!) updates to electronic medical records and insurance company software.

It also changed how we diagnose patients. When someone comes in with heart failure, we now have to note whether it's diastolic heart failure, systolic heart failure, or heart failure due to another condition. Sometimes, we don't know the information they now demand, or not without additional testing.

If someone comes into a clinic and we note their condition

as heart failure without specifying the cause according to the specific ICD-10 code, payers may not recognize our diagnosis in their list of things to treat, and may therefore decline to pay. We submitted our "solution" to the math problem, but they found an error and rejected our work.

When dealing with Medicare (and, in some states, Medicaid) plans, you must accurately code diagnostics, since these programs reimburse hospitals based on the diagnosis-related groups (MS-DRGs or APR-DRGs). In short, the more severe or complex the illness or injury, the more the hospital gets paid. If you inaccurately code diagnostics, you and your facility may not get adequately reimbursed.

EVALUATION AND MANAGEMENT

When it comes to what we *do* about the diagnosis, that's coded differently. The first step involves talking to the patient, either in the clinic, the emergency department, or the hospital. These encounters are tracked using evaluation and management (E&M) code.

In clinical notes, we record how much work we do during a patient visit. This translates into an E&M code reflecting the level of care provided, the service location, and whether patients are new or established.

Complexity is determined by the number of problems; if the problems are acute, chronic, or life-threatening; the amount of data reviewed; and the level of medical decision making needed to assess the problems. This was simplified in 2021 (outpatient) and 2023 (inpatient).

PROCEDURES

Finally, when you schedule an operation or other procedure, you put in an order for the work you're going to do using the Current Procedural Terminology (CPT) code.

The CPT code is a national language determined by the CPT editorial board appointed by the American Medical Association Board of Trustees, often in collaboration with CMS. This one is copyright protected, so you or your hospital or practice must buy the codebook or pay for an annually updated digital subscription.

AVOIDING COMMON PITFALLS

During residency you'll hear spotty mention of coding—often related to diagnosis. After all, the (faulty) logic goes, why waste time on administrative matters? As more doctors become employed by larger hospitals, we tend to think of the revenue cycle as "the hospital's problem"...until it becomes ours.

Since clinical notes inform coding—and inaccurate coding based on poor notes can result in denied, delayed, or incomplete physician reimbursements—you don't have to be running your own practice for this to become your problem. It can even become a potential fraud situation (read: *big* problem) if the incorrect code you submitted has a higher reimbursement.

If you want to know what's going on with your money, it's on you to figure it out. You can either dive in with little resistance, saving energy and time—or, you can resist, then still have to do it.

To make matters worse, if hospitals and physicians don't get paid, patients are also out of luck. Again, we can get mad about the system's complexities, or we can recognize that, like it or not, this is currently the system we need to understand. To clarify, here are some key terms.

MEDICAL NECESSITY

Medical necessity is determined by pairing of the ICD-10 with the E&M and CPT codes. Payers will not reimburse you if these don't match, because their contract stipulates they cover only those items all parties agree are medically necessary. (If you're employed, you may not see this contract; it's signed on your behalf.)

DOCUMENTATION

As far as payers are concerned, if you didn't document it, it didn't happen.

Maybe you talk to a patient and convince them to quit smoking. There's a code you can add to your visit to document—and get paid for—that work. But if you don't document it, or you do it incorrectly, you won't get compensated. You can't just say, "I counseled someone to quit smoking." You have to also estimate how many minutes you spent doing so.

Yes, these details and stipulations can cause resentment of both private and government payers, but it's nothing personal. Everyone has a business to run, so don't hate the player; hate the game.

Actually, don't even hate the game—not when you can learn the rules and play to win.

FRAUD RISK AND CHART AUDITS

When you improperly document your clinical notes, coders are not allowed to ask leading questions or fix your problems for you. It's not their job to "make it legal." It is *your* job to understand how coding works and provide supporting documentation.

That's why it's vital to have a close working relationship with coders and talk to them regularly *in person*. Coders can submit queries to you, but if there's any paper trail of them counseling you about how to increase reimbursement through using different codes, insurance auditors could accuse you both of fraud. Fraud charges can result in termination, heavy fines, and legal prosecution. Coders are here to help us, but their training rightfully advises them to protect themselves, too.

Understanding this—that far from being difficult or opaque, coders protect everyone involved from legal repercussions—goes a long way to improving your relationship with them. For a practice to function as a well-oiled machine, you need teamwork, including sufficient oversight.

I cannot overemphasize the importance of regular chart audits. Typically, these are done by an outside consultant your organization hires to spot check whether everyone's using and properly documenting the right codes. While this can get expensive, it's typically much cheaper than fraud charges and subsequent legal fees, investigations, and potentially heavy fines.

BUNDLING

Bundling combines codes related to the same work—either multiple parts of a procedure or multiple visits related to the same issue—to simplify billing.

Bundled CPT codes for one surgery might include incision and closure, as well as lysis of adhesions. There are standard bundles for particular surgeries, unless you can document additional work needed above the normal procedure. Such add-ons are considered "incidental" to the original procedure.

The E&M codes for multiple visits related to one issue get bundled too, within a global period. You might bundle multiple visits in one day under a zero-day global period, and multiple visits for a colectomy under a ninety-day bundle.

Sometimes modifiers get applied to "unbundle" codes, which can either raise or lower reimbursement. If you unbundle, make 100 percent sure you're allowed to do so; otherwise the federal government may consider it a violation of the False Claims Act, which exposes you to liability.

MODIFIERS

Let's say an auto repair shop needs to change your muffler. First, they'll estimate how much it will cost for parts and labor, based on what they know about your car. After they've done the work, they may end up charging more because they encountered related problems, which took another two hours to fix.

When this happens in medicine, we code those extra costs as "modifiers." These can be used to legally unbundle and clarify code to add another procedure. If I perform a bilateral mastectomy, I'll unbundle the code for each side. That way, the patient avoids having to pay double for something that requires neither twice the work nor twice the recovery time (global period).

Maybe a lumpectomy was harder than you thought because the size or shape presents a rare challenge, so you add a CPT code for a complex closure. Maybe a supplementary surgeon gets called in, increasing the cost of an operation. Adding a modifier code helps protect the patient from paying twice as much for that extra surgeon.

Let's say you were that supplementary surgeon called. You later realize you weren't paid the full amount you normally get when you're the only surgeon there. This may not seem fair at first, but look at the bigger picture. If the end goal is to provide the best patient experience, you wouldn't want them unexpectedly paying double. The modifier helps ensure a more fair price on both sides.

Modifiers add a layer of flexibility for procedures that require more or less than what's included in the bundle. They also introduce more complexity and risk; if we code them wrong, insurance may refuse to pay—or they may do an audit. This ends up costing the hospital, impacting physician pay down the line.

EXCLUSIVITY

In coding, the term "exclusivity" relates to procedures that cannot be coded together. The National Correct Coding Initiative (NCCI) stipulates that when coding for more than one procedure, the extra procedure coded must represent appropriate additional work not included in the original procedure.

You can't code a fracture repair along with an amputation, just as you can't code a laparoscopy with an open procedure.

RESISTANCE IS FUTILE

Instead of assuming the system is set up to screw you, try on the idea that there are at least *some* ways the system wants to reward you for work.

Think of it like taxes. No one loves the tax man, but Uncle Sam does reward us with tax credits for buying homes, starting businesses, making charitable donations, and using clean energy resources. We often demonize the IRS as complicated and onerous, but there *are* ways the system's complexities reward us for additional work.

Likewise, you may never love the medical reimbursement system, but you can shift your attitude to a neutral stance. There's no benefit to the "unknown boogeyman" narrative, but there's a lot to gain from learning the rules.

Recently, as I waited to pick up my daughter from a haunted house, I decided to confront my own fears: figuring out how to code the standards. As a private practice surgeon, determining the "right code" to avoid fraud charges or underpayment initially caused more clinic-related stress than anything else. I didn't want to deal with any of this, but in the end, I put in thirty minutes—and figured it out! Now I'll always have that practical knowledge. The effect was both freeing and empowering.

As BOSS MDs, let's drop the drama, accept reality, and get organized.

Next, we'll apply this same mindset to understanding how medical codes translate into us getting paid. Chapter 14 explores the contracts that providers have with insurance companies, including how those payers apply relative value units to the work we do, and how RVUs get us paid.

NEXT STEPS

1. Create cheat sheets for your most frequently used CPT codes and modifiers (your coder can likely run a report).
2. Ask your coders for regular, in-person feedback on notes.
3. Learn who does chart audits for your practice or hospitals and how often. Ask to see an analysis of audits over time.

RESOURCES:

AMA guide to CPT codes: https://www.ama-assn.org/practice-management/cpt

CMS list of CPT and HCPCS codes: https://www.cms.gov/medicare/fraud-and-abuse/physicianselfreferral/list_of_codes

BOSS PODCAST EPISODES:

https://www.BOSSsurgery.com/podcasts/boss-business-of-surgery-series

Ep. 53: *The Revenue Cycle, with Dr. Heather Signarelli, Founder of RevMD*

CHAPTER 14

GETTING PAID

As she looks over her personal finances, Julia realizes that—yet again—she overestimated her projected income. Since she isn't getting her expected bonus, she can't hit her savings target for the month. *Might be better to charge that surprise car repair to a credit card*, she thinks.

Julia feels caught in a loop of not earning enough to sustain her financial goals and lifestyle habits. Plus, there's the added stress of not knowing *why* her paychecks don't match her expectations.

"Who understands any of this?!" Julia shouts to her home computer screen, startling her cat. Frustrated, she walks away from the spreadsheets and bank apps and starts on dinner. While dicing tomatoes, Julia realizes: *That's a good question actually. Who can explain what I need to know?*

If, like Julia, you feel confused, overworked, and underpaid, it can feel like you-against-the-world. This accelerates physician burnout and overwhelm. But the truth is, when it comes to understanding the medical money cycle, you don't have to go it alone.

You work alongside people who specialize in medical coding, as well as billing and reimbursement. Far from some nameless, faceless system, there's a pathway from electronic medical records to physician reimbursements—all populated by human professionals.

Sometimes, we're invited to meet with medical coders or billers. When this happens, it can feel like more work—or a punishment. But talking to these folks actually provides a productive opportunity to learn about systems at play—and build more efficiency and collaboration into the reimbursement process.

This chapter reintroduces you to the human players related to coding, billing, and reimbursement. We'll also unpack how RVUs translate into those numbers you see on your paycheck.

PLAYERS IN THE PROCESS

If you never want to personally code a clinical note, you may prefer to work as an employed doctor at a hospital with paid medical coders who translate notes into codes. However (per Chapter 13), it's still better to understand the system so you can avoid omissions and errors in your notes. (Remember, if there's a hit to your license or NPI number, regardless if you or your coder's to blame, that's a hit to you.)

Even if you think you're coding the notes, there's often a coder in the background checking—and maybe changing—your work, to protect you and the hospital from fraud and underpayment. But they don't know the medical details you do. I had a coder add a modifier to decrease a payment for a gallbladder surgery because "the gallbladder wasn't completely removed." She did not understand that a subtotal cholecystectomy was exponentially *more* work, not less. If I hadn't spoken to her, I might not have known I was getting underpaid.

Find out who to talk to and what questions to ask when your check ends up slimmer than you thought. Instead of assuming admin's ripping you off, talk to your coders to make sure you're giving them what they need. Again, the system's made up of people—who are there to help.

If you ever launch a private practice, make sure to hire—and thoroughly train—top-quality coders and billers. You will put a lot of trust, financial and otherwise, on these staff members to ensure your practice gets fairly reimbursed and stays out of trouble. You'll also want to audit regularly.

CODERS

Coders find and code billable services from clinical notes and supporting documents we provide. They're typically not medically trained. They simply review clinical notes for diagnoses, evaluations, and procedures, then they match those to the relevant codes from a codebook.

Coders are legally not permitted to edit our notes, fill in gaps, or assume anything. They can only code according to the information we provide to them—so it's on *us* to give them clear, accurate, and thorough information.

I've gotten pretty good at asking my coders questions: *Am I documenting everything correctly? Am I missing opportunities to get compensated for work?*

When I mess up, they tell me (verbally) and I change it. They'll say something like, "If you add this sentence to your dictation, you can go to a different, applicable code that helps us understand better what you did and code it right."

As you know, the right side of a colon connects to the ileocecal valve. If you remove the right colon, that valve comes too. But did you know there's a separate CPT code for the removal of ileocecal valve—and you get more money when you take that out too?

Admittedly, that doesn't make much sense. If I didn't know this, I would neglect to mention the removal of this valve in my clinical notes. Meanwhile, the coder may not know these procedures automatically go together. Even if they did, if *I* don't explicitly mention the valve removal in my notes, coders legally cannot code it without risking fraud charges.

BILLERS

Billers use specific software to submit codes with supporting documentation to prove medical necessity. The software sends claims to payers either directly or through a clearinghouse.

Billers submit claims using the CMS-1500 claim form, which involves three parts: (1) Patient information, (2) Procedure and diagnostic information (codes), and (3) Provider information.

Billers also typically explain charges to patients. In other words, they're used to breaking this down—and typically, they're more than happy to answer physician questions as well.

AUDITORS

Medical coding auditors examine your coding, documentation, billing claims, and reimbursements to ensure that everything matches up and complies with payer contracts and/or federal regulations.

Most large hospitals and medical systems employ internal auditors within their compliance office. For private practice physicians, it's a good idea to contract with someone to run quarterly—or at least annual—audits for you. This helps maintain good medical coding and billing hygiene—and prepares you to ace any unexpected external audits from private or government payers.

Like the IRS, payers often audit hospitals or practices in response to red flags. For example, if your clinic consistently submits claims for disproportionate volumes of high level care, it's likely to attract attention.

You should also prepare for random external audits. Even a low-income provider can face serious consequences for a minor oversight, such as not appropriately tracking the time for a clinical encounter. Coding and billing mistakes can escalate to fraud charges, resulting in heavy fines and fees, or even revocation of your license.

Learning the ins and outs of the money cycle and running internal audits can feel tedious. But we all understand the health benefits of preventive care and regular screenings. The same applies to your coding and billing.

Once again, you have a choice: Either live in fear of an external audit, or educate yourself and get prepared.

RELATIVE VALUE UNITS

Once payers approve invoices, they assign different relative value units (RVUs) to each E&M and CPT code. Maybe an office visit gets three RVUs, but if I take your colon out, that's worth twenty-five. This system assesses and standardizes everything we do, based on how much things cost relative to the broader system of medicine.

There are two kinds of RVUs: *work* relative value units (wRVUs) measuring the amount of work done by physician providers, and facility relative value units (fRVUs) measuring costs incurred by the medical facility. This chapter focuses on the former, wRVUs (we'll deal with fRVUs in Chapter 16).

The sum of your wRVUs for each pay period can seem mysterious, since your paycheck doesn't include an itemized list of how your work converts to RVUs. It just adds up the clinical and procedural volume based on E&M and CPT codes, then spits out a sum.

If you want to do the math yourself, it tends to be quite predictable. Track all the cases you did this month, maybe consult with your coders or billers to clarify or confirm, and you can calculate your own wRVUs based on relevant E&M and CPT codes. Less predictable is the effect that modifiers have on these codes, but you can still get within range without these calculations until you learn more.

PHYSICIAN REIMBURSEMENTS

While RVUs are standardized, how those translate into physician pay varies by region, community, and practice. In a Midwestern rural community, wRVUs for hernia repair may convert to $500. Meanwhile, in Boston—where cost of living and operating a practice is much higher—it may be $1,200.

Even within the same geographic region, physician pay varies from one practice to the next, based on the facility's size, services provided, insurance payer mix, and what they consider to be fair, competitive pay.

In other words, employers have wiggle room, which they sometimes use to incentivize productivity. After hiring you, they may say, "Do this number of cases, and we'll pay you X amount per wRVU up to Y amount of work. If you do extra, we'll increase the pay per wRVU."

Whether you're underpaid (based on patients and revenue you bring in) or overpaid (and therefore at risk of losing your job in an unsustainable system), you can't afford to not understand what's going on.

YOUR ROLE IN THE MONEY CYCLE

If you understand your role in the money cycle, you can influence it, like the BOSS MD you are. First, drop the pointless resistance and resentment currently eroding your bandwidth.

Yes, it's complicated, and the details can bog you down. Start with the big-picture mechanics and basic principles. The more you understand, the less likely you'll be to commit errors and oversights on clinical notes, coding, and billing. These concepts are not unique to medicine. For almost any work, you'd need to estimate a job, provide an invoice to show your work, and collect.

As an employed physician, you may not be directly involved in setting up insurance contracts, coding, or billing, but you can and should build relationships with coders, billers, and other administrators. When it comes to getting paid, they are your allies, not your adversaries.

Take some time to study the language of coding, billing, and insurance contracts. As Julia experienced with her personal finances, a lot of discomfort comes down to simply not understanding basic system mechanics. Get curious, gather as much info as possible, and figure out your place in it all—i.e., what you can change, versus when and how to adapt.

As Julia begins to demystify the vagaries of billing and reimbursement for herself, she notices a similar pattern of confusion and frustration among her patients when it comes to their insurance contracts.

The next chapter will dive deeper into how insurance contracts work, and how common misunderstandings about patient-payer agreements impact your practice and your pay.

NEXT STEPS

1. Get to know your billers, coders, compliance officers, and other money cycle players.
2. Set up quarterly meetings with them to learn how you can better support their work.

CHAPTER 15

INSURANCE PITFALLS

Since delegating more collaboratively with support staff, Julia got her clinical schedule on track. Still, delays happen. First thing this morning, a tangent into the complexities of patient insurance prolonged one of her clinical visits, throwing off the rest of her day.

The patient angrily complained about his medical bill, since he expected co-payments related to his care to count toward his annual deductible. When Julia tried to explain, the patient got defensive—prompting a similar reaction in Julia, which she tried to suppress.

Looking back, Julia realizes that when it comes to insurance issues, she's probably defensive because, in many ways, she's in the same boat as patients. Doctors and patients alike get bogged down by the laborious details of medical insurance contracts. Plus, when patients can't pay their end, it impacts our pay. Besides, not only do we not choose our patients' insurance agreements, there's also nothing we can do to change them, legally or practically.

In the thorny world of medical insurance, it's important to appreciate the different sets of legal agreements involved, how they work, and why. This chapter provides an overview of how insurance works, what happens when things go wrong, and your role in helping your patients understand.

THE HOUSE ALWAYS WINS

As physicians, we function within a service oriented industry. In other service industries—say, plumbing—contracts are more simple. You notice a problem with your pipes, call the plumber, and set up a contract directly with them.

Similarly, a patient notices a health problem and calls the doctor. Unlike the plumber, our services are more expensive than the average patient can afford, so instead of signing a contract directly with us for our services, they've previously set up a contract with an insurance company.

We typically accept patients (and/or they choose us) based on whether or not they're "in network," which means we have our own contract with their same insurance company. The patient's contract states something like, "If you (patient) have X problem, we (insurance company) will pay Y amount." Meanwhile our contract states something like, "I (physician) will treat X problem for your customer, and you (insurance company) will pay me Y amount on their behalf."

We know that insurance contracts are much more complicated

than anything a plumber might send to a client. Let's examine some of the risks, laws, and limitations to better understand why private and government payers represent "the house"—and the house always wins.

LIMITATIONS

In an ideal world, the patient chooses an insurance contract best suited to meet their particular needs and means. Unfortunately, average Americans face serious limitations when it comes to their ability to meaningfully choose. Most accept whatever insurance company has contracted with their employer, choosing among a small set of plan options. Marketplace health plans for individuals can't really compete with company plans, in terms of either coverage or affordability.

That doesn't change the fact that we, as physicians, have literally *zero* ability to choose or change anything about our patients' insurance contracts. While we have some degree of choice over which payers we contract with, we face limitations too.

No matter what, both providers and patients must understand the responsibilities and agreements stipulated in their respective legal contracts.

FRAUD RISK

As mentioned in Chapter 14, private and government payers hire auditors to assess claims for potential fraud. Some external auditors, especially those who work for the federal government, earn a percentage of their fraud collections, incentivizing legal action. Read the fine print on your contracts, and learn to collaborate with your coders, billers, and hospital compliance officers—they're there to protect you and your practice.

Yes, it gets confusing and frustrating. You'd be forgiven for concluding that the system is awful and rigged against both us and the patients we've vowed to serve. In short, both insurance companies and CMS represent the house, and the house always wins.

While that may sound discouraging, let's get realistic about current limitations, complexities, and misconceptions surrounding payers in general. Not only does this make you more savvy about your own insurance contracts, it can also help you clarify what's going on for your patients.

EMTALA AND NO SURPRISES ACT

Congress passed the Emergency Treatment and Labor Act (EMTALA) in 1986 to prohibit transfer from one hospital to another due to a patient's inability to pay. If doctors are able to care for a patient but nevertheless decline admission, they violate the law and subject the hospital to fines.

The No Surprises Act passed in 2022 to ensure healthcare price transparency. This law protects patients from surprise bills for emergency services at out-of-network facilities or from out-of-network providers at in-network facilities, holding patients responsible only for in-network cost-sharing amounts (like copay and coinsurance).

Part II of the No Surprise Act expanded billing regulations to require all providers and health care facilities licensed, certified, or approved by the state to provide good faith estimates of expected charges for services and items offered to uninsured and self-pay consumers.

If a patient with an out-of-network plan comes into the emergency department with acute appendicitis, for example, we must offer them a choice: "We can see you now, or transfer you at your expense." This puts the burden on providers to figure out the patient's insurance situation versus the person who actually chose the contract.

COMMON MISCONCEPTIONS

The first misunderstanding our patients tend to have is appreciating that there are two basic dynamics in place: (1) The patient's insurance contract, and (2) The doctor's insurance contract.

When we ask a patient for their copay, this charge may go toward paying us, but it's not set up by us. Their insurance company previously arranged the terms of this transaction, and the patient agreed to it. As physicians, we're as subject to the terms of patients' contracts as they are.

While it's not our obligation to help patients understand the plan they chose, it can be a good idea. Not just for courtesy, but also because when patients understand their insurance contracts, they're more likely to pay their share—so we're more likely to get ours.

COPAY

Patients often conflate the cost of their copay with the cost of the entire doctor's visit. That visit may end up costing the hospital

$200, with the patient paying their $20 copay, and the insurance company paying the rest. Meanwhile, someone who chose a different plan may pay a $50 copay for the same visit.

As doctors, we didn't decide to charge different rates to different people, nor did our administrators. We legally cannot renegotiate anything about the situation without violating a legally binding contract between patient and insurance company.

If we try to waive part or all of a copay, we're either committing insurance fraud or, in the case of a Medicare patient, violating the law. That's because, as part of our separate contracts with insurance companies, we've agreed to help payers recoup money by enforcing the terms of our contracts. Medicare makes it abundantly clear that waiving co-pays and deductibles is a no-go.

In short, while medical ethics—not to mention legal requirements for publicly funded hospitals—do not allow us to refuse care to patients, hospitals also have to pay for equipment, supplies, and professional services. If we can't afford to pay our bills and provide services, everyone loses.

COINSURANCE VERSUS COPAY

Confusion often arises when patients check into a hospital for an extended period of time, say overnight. They may think they have to pay just coinsurance for their hospital stay and procedures, not realizing there's also a $20 copay for each related physician encounter.

If a doctor visits the hospitalized patient three times during the course of their stay, the patient gets charged $60 for physician compensation. Meanwhile, the patient's coinsurance gets separately applied to hospital fees.

DEDUCTIBLES

Deductibles represent the amount patients must pay out of pocket before their insurance company starts to pick up the bill. Many patients assume that any and all medical services (except free preventive services) go toward their deductible.

Unfortunately—especially for those with high deductible plans— many plans exclude certain services from counting toward the deductible. Patients should closely read their policy information or speak to an insurance representative to learn more.

PHYSICIAN CONTRACTS

Just as patients can choose insurance contracts poorly, physicians can too. Say one insurance company pays me $800 to take out a gallbladder, another pays me $1200, and yet a third pays only $600. In all three cases, we use the same current procedural terminology (CPT) code, but the terms of our contracts determine how that code translates into our pay.

Most specialists operate through referrals. Before a new patient sets up an appointment, we must make sure their insurance company is in network, meaning that we also have an agreement with that company.

As a courtesy, it can help to make sure patients understand their own responsibilities, especially in terms of upfront copay—essentially a shared down payment—and subsequent coinsurance, determined later by the level of evaluations and procedures performed, coded, then billed for reimbursement based on our notes and electronic medical records.

Insurance delays can arise when insurance companies require patients to use their deductibles before they'll pay coinsurance. If an ER patient has $500 left on their deductible and their procedure costs $1000, the hospital has to first collect the $500. After the deductible is met, things get easier because we can then go straight to the payer.

There's a wide range of managed care plans—and a vat of alphabet soup that goes along with them: HMO, PPO, POS, and so on. As a provider, you're responsible for the terms of your own contracts, and your patients are responsible for their own.

It can help to join forces with other groups, either an accountable care organization (ACO) or other hospital organization, to negotiate higher-paying insurance contracts for all. There's power in numbers.

All the contracts we choose as providers—known as our payer mix—impact the annual revenue of our practices. We'll get into more depth about how payer mix and other factors impact clinical finances in the next chapter.

MINDSET SHIFTS

As an employed physician, you may not have a complete understanding of your employers' contract with insurance companies. To better understand how you're paid, find out more about your payer mix—specifically the ratio of private insurance payers to government payers accepted by your practice and represented by your current patient population.

This can factor into job-hunting. As discussed in Chapter 2, surgeons practicing in an affluent area can easily earn twice as much as those serving a rural or lower-income urban population, mainly because government payers tend to reimburse much less than private insurance. Most physicians just want to help people, but it certainly takes a toll to work twice as hard and earn the same or less than colleagues practicing in a different area.

Earlier I used a casino reference to describe payers—"the house always wins." But while we can (and should) argue about how much private payers profit from our medical system, they have a business to run too. Everyone has to get paid along the way.

Taking the time to educate patients upfront about insurance complexities can help ensure they pay what they agreed to. It also helps avoid patient frustration—such as Julia's disgruntled patient complaining about hospital bills.

In addition to unpacking terms like copay, coinsurance, and deductible, keep patient expectations realistic. Our insurance system in the US isn't set up to save patients a ton of money on their medical care—especially those with high deductible plans. Instead, it aims to (mostly) protect patients from medical bankruptcy.

In terms of becoming the BOSS MD, you may have noticed a theme—specifically, educating yourself and understanding the limits of what you can change, then accepting and adapting to the rest. This is not to say, become complacent, but rather: Stop wasting energy and time resisting and resenting.

When it comes to insurance billing and reimbursement, the cards may be stacked against us, but we've still got legal contracts to uphold. Julia, and all of us, would do better to proactively address potential insurance concerns by making sure her patients understand their responsibilities.

In addition to the coding, billing/reimbursement, and insurance issues we've covered so far, clinics and hospitals face a lot of additional expenses. As Julia becomes more financially savvy, she's curious about how her practice manages those expenses, and how they impact her own pay. Chapter 16 breaks down the basics of clinical finances.

NEXT STEPS

1. Review your insurance contracts for details on ICD-10 and CPT coding.
2. Get to know your insurance points of contact and regularly ask them questions.
3. Talk to a practice consultant to better understand and optimize your billing and revenue cycle process.

CHAPTER 16

CLINICAL FINANCES

Julia definitely misses some things about the large hospital she worked with before moving to private practice. Namely, the equipment. Lately, she's been asking admins about upgrading the practice's handheld ultrasound machine, but they keep citing budget constraints.

When she does her own research, Julia's shocked to see the price of the machine she used at her old job. No wonder her practice hesitates to upgrade.

That's just one part of it. In addition to buying the equipment, practices pay for their highly specialized maintenance and repair. Not to mention everything else they're budgeting for: salaries and wages, rent, taxes, insurance (health, malpractice, etc.), utilities, office supplies, advertising, software, medical waste disposal, licensing fees, and more.

Next time you're concerned about your income, recognize that as a physician, your personal paycheck comprises a tiny part of this overall equation. It would take a whole book to even begin to break down the complete picture of hospital finance (and this ain't it). Instead, this chapter focuses mainly on personnel—which represents the largest expense—as well as the key revenue variable that is insurance payer mix.

PERSONNEL

If, like Julia, you're trying to get some equipment or service added to your clinic—whether small private practice or huge medical system—you'll need to demonstrate return on investment (ROI).

This is true for people, too. While a large staff can become unsustainable (especially if they're underqualified or poorly trained), sometimes growing the team can improve finances.

At my practice, I used to spend lots of time on things that don't require a surgeon, so I hired an NP to share the load. I was willing to pay more to buy back some of my time, and with less on my plate, I could focus mainly on high level work.

Plus, my NP took on revenue generating services that actually brought more money into the practice. She schedules and conducts initial evaluations, gets histories, does examinations, and gathers notes and imaging for me to review. Suddenly, clinical encounters that used to take me thirty minutes only required five minutes of my time—without losing any relationship building with patients. Now we were seeing more patients using less of my time.

At first, this caused me anxiety. Did my patients feel jilted by me, or cheated out of physician time? Shouldn't I be there to oversee everything? Ultimately though, I realized that as long as I hired and trained my nurse practitioner right, I can let go of the overwhelming urge to both control every aspect of my business and please everyone all of the time. (Which is great, because neither are realistic goals.) This led to a much better business model in which I could preserve my time and effort for work at the top of my license, while empowering those around me to also do higher level work.

Leveraging human resources effectively requires more than good hiring and training. As discussed in Part 2, good delegation and relationship management also help ensure efficient practice management and better financial sustainability.

It is possible to go too far when it comes to personnel-related solutions to financial pressures. I spoke to one physician's assistant (PA) who left a hospital emergency department that he believed hired too many advanced practice providers (or APPs, which include both NPs and PAs) to save on costs—with very little physician oversight. While APPs represent an invaluable part of the budget equation, this surgeon worried that the relative lack of physician oversight at this ER had become dangerous for patients.

Supervising an APP takes time and effort. You need to properly train and support them—reviewing charts, meeting regularly, and evaluating their progress. As discussed in Chapter 12, those investments can pay off in the long run. What's more, if you work for a larger employer, you can negotiate a supervisory stipend for this work.

You don't have to run your own practice to benefit from learning about clinical finances. If you're employed at a hospital or just starting out in a smaller practice, it helps to understand what administrators are going through.

This can shift your mindset from "Are they taking advantage of me?" to "How can I help the practice (and, by extension, myself) to spend less and earn more—without compromising on quality patient care?"

PAYER MIX

Your practice payer mix largely determines how much revenue your practice or hospital earns. This reflects the respective percentages of income earned from private insurance reimbursements, government programs like Medicaid and Medicare, and self-pay patients.

Government payers tend to reimburse less than both private insurance companies and self-pay patients. Sometimes, they even pay less than the cost of actual procedures, so if your practice accepts a lot of Medicaid or Medicare patients, your employer could end up paying you more than they get reimbursed for your work. This is true whether you're paid by variable wRVUs or a guaranteed salary.

That's not a sustainable model. If you don't bring more money into the hospital than they pay you for your services, they won't be able to afford you anymore—and you may lose your job.

One notable exception relates to federally qualified health care centers (FQHQs). These practices operate within underserved areas and therefore depend on federal subsidies to balance the budget. They tend to be community or migrant health centers that focus mainly on primary care, OB-GYN services, preventive care, and screenings. To qualify as an FQHQ, your practice must prove, through extensive documentation, that it meets strictly enforced federal requirements.

I'm writing this shortly after the federal government announced a more than 4 percent decrease in 2023 Medicare reimbursements. It's no wonder that many (especially small) practices limit their Medicare and Medicaid patients, some even outright refusing to accept government insurance plans. After all, if a practice can't maintain its bottom line, nobody gets paid.

Even as reimbursements decrease, we're often asked to do more. Researchers now recommend breast MRI screenings in addition to mammograms. Luckily, because breast cancer impacts up to one in eight women, strong advocacy groups lobby the Centers for Medicare and Medicaid to reimburse appropriately for breast cancer screenings and treatment.

Speaking of public advocacy impacting reimbursement rates, you might remember the 2014 social media "ice bucket challenge" for amyotrophic lateral sclerosis. To raise awareness of this rare but devastating disorder, people filmed themselves dumping buckets of ice water on their heads. The effort successfully raised hundreds of thousands of dollars—while also getting the attention of the CMS.

Often, when government programs cut (or increase) reimbursements, private commercial payers follow suit. That's the nature of a competition-based marketplace. They figure, *if the government's reimbursing less, we can too.*

Competition impacts the situation in other ways too. I recently spoke to a solo practice podiatrist who tried to set up a contract with Medicare but got refused because they "already had enough podiatrists" in their network. This can happen with private insurers too, when their business plan requires a narrower network with predictable practice patterns.

That said, being the only game in town doesn't necessarily give you much leverage. I recall one case involving an orthopedic surgery group. They were the only orthopedic group in their part of the state. Still, when they asked a major insurance company to increase their reimbursements—which hadn't changed in more than a decade—the insurance company dropped them in response. This left local patients insured by this company with no nearby orthopedic surgeons in network.

Payer mix has many nuanced budget implications. If yours consists of mainly high deductible private insurance plans, expect a considerable spike in (especially elective) procedures toward the end of the calendar year, when more people have met annual deductibles. (Once the deductible gets so high that people no longer expect to ever meet it, that effect tends to decrease.)

WHEN PATIENTS CAN'T PAY

We can rail against what we cannot control, but it's far more productive to figure out how to best manage in the system we currently have. To minimize the harm of systemic flaws, we must understand how the system works.

One option for practices struggling with insurance delays or financial concerns related to payer mix is to stop taking insurance altogether. This may sound extreme, but cash-based and direct primary care practices are becoming more popular, especially for elective surgeries. If every patient refused to contract with an insurance company and instead saved the amount they would pay in monthly premiums over the years, they'd usually have enough to pay out of pocket for their care—with the notable exception of costly extended care for things like cancer treatment or major injuries.

While not perfect, this approach has its perks. While patients pay more out of pocket, they tend to face fewer procedural delays and they enjoy more transparency when it comes to costs—usually in the form of flat fees. Meanwhile, practices can charge less for services while earning more. That's because they no longer need to pay additional billing staff to get preauthorizations, process claims, and collect.

This model does bring up accessibility issues, since you're limited to patients who can afford to pay out of pocket. In other words, there are three variables at play when it comes to medical care: (1) Quality, (2) Access, and (3) Affordability. Given the reality of our current medical system, medical providers can only expect to offer two out of three.

If you're not ready to drop private insurance payers, another option is to secure as much upfront payment as possible from patients. In my practice, we try our best to do this, but when someone can't afford it, we collect what we can and offer a payment plan.

While cash-based practices represent a more extreme approach, I wonder if the out-of-pocket model may catch on more as both government and private payers continue to squeeze providers. After all, if enough practices refused to accept insurance contracts, we might finally see some much-needed major changes to our system.

There are providers who try to do both; they offer insurance-based care while also providing a concierge model for patients who prefer to pay out of pocket. This gets tricky, as insurance companies want you to charge their members for services covered by their contracts. If you're considering a "hybrid" practice, make sure your contracts allow this approach—and in the case of Medicare, never charge a separate fee for any covered service.

STOP PLAYING SMALL

Like Julia, you may want your practice to invest in new equipment, or perhaps hire more staff. When making recommendations, figure out the details involved before presenting the idea to the folks who have to actually make financial decisions impacting everyone.

You may think, "Why don't we just share the MRI machine— or even clinical space—with physicians from the practice next door?" The answer may not be that your administration lacks creativity and innovation. There are also fraud and anti-kickback rules to consider when it comes to referrals and rental agreements. Solutions are rarely as simple as they first appear.

The good news is that, once you start thinking this way, you'll learn a lot about clinical finances. This will increase your profile at work and your influence over the direction of your practice.

Instead of feeling like the victim, you're growing into a BOSS MD who's earned a prominent place at the table—a valuable partner and advocate for the practice. Maybe the future CEO of your own practice. It certainly doesn't hurt to ask yourself: *If I were running the show, what would I do, and why? How could I reduce costs or better allocate resources?*

As Julia's learned, appreciating both the benefits and drawbacks of the status quo is the first step toward improving things. She decided to track the ultrasound procedures she performed at her practice and calculate related reimbursements to determine which piece of equipment her practice can afford. While she wasn't able to get the one she really wanted, she made a convincing argument and soon got upgraded equipment.

By educating herself about the money cycle, Julia's learned to improve outcomes and increase returns for the whole team. By gaining influence within her practice, she's beginning to realize the power she has to evolve within her current role, and possibly expand into different professional options.

It all starts with appreciating the interconnected larger systems and structures in place—including what you can and cannot change. Practices may have limited control over revenue related to payer mix, but a lot can be done in terms of time and energy. If allocated right, these resources translate into substantial money savings, but time and energy are invaluable in and of themselves.

In fact, if you ask me, they're the most precious resources of all. Part 5, on protecting your assets, tackles how to best protect and leverage these resources throughout your medical career.

NEXT STEPS

1. Research ROI before suggesting or investing in new equipment or personnel.
2. Analyze the payer mix of patients in your community.
3. Consider what practice model (cash-based, hybrid, or insurance-based) would work best in your community.

BOSS PODCAST EPISODES:

https://www.BOSSsurgery.com/podcasts/
boss-business-of-surgery-series

Ep. 42: *Dropping the Safety Nets of Employment and Insurance, with Dr. Tea Nguyen*

Ep. 47: *Succeeding in Private Practice, with Dr. Jenna Kazil*

Ep. 48: *Starting a Cash-Based Surgery Practice, with Dr. Cheruba Prabakar*

PART 5

PROTECT YOUR ASSETS

CHAPTER 17

DEFICIT MINDSET

Julia's establishing herself as a senior partner. She recently got a substantial raise, took on a more official supervisory role, and hired a PA to help support her patients. As she evolves professionally, Julia sacrifices much less energy to interpersonal dramas, victim narratives, and procrastination-overcompensation cycles.

So, why do most days still feel like a hustle?

The truth is that, despite feeling more empowered professionally, Julia's still generally exhausted. It constantly feels like there's never enough time to do everything at work and home.

That's in part because life keeps changing. Julia recently got married and purchased a home with her husband, Rob. As her thirties wane, she feels the pressures of family planning—but even considering having kids feels stressful. Life is hectic enough! Plus, Julia's still paying off medical education debts, in addition to this new mortgage. Can she and her husband even afford kids?

This kind of thinking exemplifies what I call the "deficit mindset." That relentless, over-thinking hustle energy, predicated on one basic fear: "I don't have enough!" Deficit mindset loves to worry about resources—time, money, energy, skill. It can convert any potential solution into something new to worry about.

Julia hired her PA to take some pressure off her schedule—but now she's grinding her gears about how to find time to train the new person and whether they can budget for the additional overhead. The deficit mindset can become a black hole that, far from solving our problems, only perpetuates and reinforces the sense of deficiency. Mainly because it's rooted in worry, and worry doesn't add value. It only detracts and drains, costing us vital energy and focus that impairs our ability to succeed.

Julia may be advancing in her career—learning new professional skills like budgeting and management, but each time she levels up, her deficit mindset pops in with new fears—or perhaps more accurately, new variations on the age-old fear of lack: Not enough time. Not enough money. Not enough energy to get it all done.

Part 4 summarized how financial resources flow through the reimbursement cycle. But money is only one part of the equation. The rest of the book will discuss how to leverage knowledge and influence to protect our most precious resources: time and energy.

The relentless pace and competition of residency and clinical work—not to mention the very real weight of educational debt—all help lock physicians into the deficit mindset. Without the right perspective and life-work balance, burn-out will keep pulling us back.

Living life with a deficit mindset influences career choices in unconscious, disempowering ways. This chapter revisits themes from earlier in the book—mainly, that we have command over our own beliefs. As BOSS MDs, we can become the heroes of our own stories by choosing a mindset that empowers us to take back our time and energy.

WORRY IS A CHOICE

When we think we may not have enough, we worry. Like Julia, many of us constantly churn through *what ifs* and *maybes*—all leading toward some imaginary collapse of resources.

Deficit mindset insists you're not doing enough. It convinces you it's productive or responsible to fret about hypothetical problems or constantly compare yourself to some unattainable ideal.

It's not. In fact, worry doesn't produce much value at all. To some extent, it can help fuel efforts, ensuring you get things done and get paid—but worry demands a high energy cost. As with any expensive fuel, you'll soon get diminishing returns.

As discussed in Chapter 1, thoughts and beliefs become patterns that influence our behavior and our experience of the world. We can do this unconsciously, or we can begin to notice our habits and consciously choose new patterns—ones that do not cost us our ability to succeed.

Say it's a light time of year in terms of clinical scheduling, maybe the first few weeks of a new year. You can convince yourself your patients have abandoned you and you won't be able to pay the bills—or, you can recall that some times of year are busier than others. Sometimes your clinic is full; sometimes it's not. There's a natural rhythm to patient flow, but if we don't recognize that down times are normal, expected, and even predictable, we can drive ourselves to distraction. Instead, use this precious time to accomplish other goals you've been putting off.

When I hired my NP full time, I knew it was a good idea. I even demonstrated to myself that it was a good idea, not only based on my newfound ability to focus on the higher level work I most enjoy, but also based on our healthy bottom line. Even still, I worried.

I kept tricking myself into thinking I still had to personally do and fix everything. On one hand, it's true that I'm responsible for everything that happens in my clinic. But taking ownership as a leader doesn't mean doing it all yourself. You're most susceptible to a deficit mindset when you believe the world rests on your shoulders, because truly, you don't have enough time or energy to carry everything. No one does.

UNANSWERED QUESTIONS

How we interpret reality is a choice. If your mind keeps spiraling back to: "Is this enough?"—good news! You get to answer that question for yourself!

I believe most of our worry and overwhelm comes from unanswered questions stealing our energy. Simply ask—and answer—the questions, and you can usually stop the spinning. "Do we have enough patients in this clinic? What happens if we don't hit our monthly budget goal?"

Try answering your questions in multiple ways. You'll need data, but also pay attention to how each answer feels. You could sit down with only cold, hard facts and decide, "If we increase patients by this much, we can make that much." However, you have to also ask, "Is that a reasonable goal? Can our human resources support it? What is the sweet spot between ideal revenue and what's possible?"

One thing's for sure: You're not going to come up with actionable answers if all you do is sit and worry and binge eat from stress—or whatever maladaptive coping mechanism your brain comes up with to deal with your deficit mindset. The answer to the worry doesn't lie at the bottom of the bag of chips. Instead, start by asking yourself: *What am I actually worried about?*

One question I keep coming back to—even while I'm doing surgery, directing a private practice, running a side business coaching, and podcasting—is always this: "Am I doing enough?"

That unanswered question caused me untold stress—until I began to consciously ask and answer it. What I learned surprised me. I learned that the answer is always "Yes—and…"

Yes, I am doing enough with what I have right now—and, I still want to grow and try harder. Most of the time, both answers are true.

That said, not every single time. Sometimes I'm legitimately not doing enough, and other times, I'm certainly trying to do too much. One workload may be more than enough when your infant child or aging parent needs care. Other times, you can comfortably add more.

Just remember that one light clinic week doesn't mean everything's about to fall apart. Nor does worrying and catastrophizing help the situation. It also doesn't help to mindlessly tire yourself out by just working extra hard without clear goals or boundaries—just because anxiety told you to.

EMBRACE DOWNTIME

Hustle is easy. It's just work—and we're good at that, right? Often though, the extra hustle is not only unnecessary, it's actively draining your time and energy.

Once you get trapped in the deficit mindset, that sense of lack becomes a black hole we try to fill by working harder. However, life is very rarely the zero-sum game we think it is. If we never allow ourselves to step off the hamster wheel, we'll never see it.

As an antidote to mindless hustle, consciously build white space into your schedule. Insist on spacing outpatient visits by at least ten minutes to ensure time to finish clinical notes. Refuse to take meetings on Fridays. Hire support, or even—as I've done and will discuss more in Chapter 20—build in regular days off to review, relax, and strategize.

Physicians tend to be highly educated high earners who never feel like we deserve any down time. We set ourselves up in unsustainable practices, because that's what we're used to. When that doesn't work, we simultaneously villainize and victimize ourselves: *It's all my fault. But also: I can't do everything!*

Some math problems can't be solved by constantly adding. Sometimes, we have to subtract in order to gain. When it feels like we're drowning, the answer is not to do more. That only sets you up for proving that the problem is either the work itself or our inability to "do it all"—rather than our thoughts about the work.

We need to tell ourselves the truth about what's possible in a day. That may mean making decisions about not doing something we want to do. The goal is to become the creator of your time, not the reactor to it. This comes down to establishing boundaries around time and effort.

THE FOUR STEPS OF BOUNDARY SETTING

Boundaries sometimes get a bad name, especially when we operate from a deficit mindset. The idea of imposing limits on others can raise all kinds of negative self-talk. We worry we're being selfish by taking something away from others, or about what might happen if we stop people-pleasing.

True boundaries foster mutual understanding that builds relationships through being honest about what we need, clearly communicating those needs to others, and planning in advance what we'll do if the boundary is violated.

There are four steps to every boundary:

1. Identifying what the boundary is, and why.

2. Communicating that boundary to others—and to yourself.
3. Establishing what happens if that boundary is violated (even by you).
4. Actually following through with steps 1–4.

Bonus step five: If you choose to occasionally cross your own boundary, that's okay—if you're happy with your reasons. If you're constantly violating your boundaries (or allowing others to), I would revisit all four steps to evaluate whether or not you're being honest with yourself and others about both what you need and what's possible.

Your boundaries are your prerogative. Like clinical notes, think of them as a helpful tool, not as another obligatory task. The purpose of boundaries is to protect your energy and your time. The trouble is that most of us don't even do the first step of articulating our boundaries—even to ourselves.

How you spend time in a clinical encounter can be a boundary issue you have with others—but also with *yourself*. As discussed in Chapter 11, I recommend keeping clinical work—including your notes—in the clinic. But realistically speaking, note taking will occasionally spill over past your visit, even if you keep them bare-bones outline. A complementary boundary could ensure your schedule builds in ten to fifteen minutes between appointments to finish notes. That's step one: identify the boundary.

Step two—communicate this scheduling boundary—could entail asking office staff not to book back-to-back appointments. You can also make sure you're not violating your own boundary by letting patients drone on, eating up your buffer zone between visits. Instead, alert each patient that you'll need to end the visit precisely fifteen minutes before the hour.

When the boundary gets crossed (step three), you have options. If a patient keeps talking, you can set up another appointment to address concerns at a later time. Or, you can simply decline to move on to the next patient until you at least have an outline for the rest of your notes.

Make sure you consistently follow through with steps one through three. This trains both you and others to take your boundaries seriously. Otherwise, they lose all meaning.

Maybe your boundary is to keep clinical scheduling to twenty or fewer patients per day. You've done the math and determined that twenty patients a day will pay the bills without burning everyone out. This model preserves time and effort.

Say you've communicated the boundary to staff—but then they see you schedule additional patients within the first week. By immediately crossing your own boundary you send mixed messages, leading to more boundary violations. Instead, have a plan: If more than twenty people get booked (even by you), have administrators reschedule.

Again, if they're your boundaries, it's okay to occasionally cross them—provided you like your reasons and can communicate those. Just keep exceptions few and well justified.

AIM FOR BALANCE

With so much going on, Julia indulged in some directionless

worry. Even after making a good choice—hiring a PA—she found new things to worry about ("How will I afford the overhead?"). This led back to her default setting of mindless hustle, which set a poor example for her team, making everyone else feel like they needed to overwork.

Eventually though, Julia asked herself the right questions, collaborated with her team on a plan, and put it into action—like the BOSS MD she is. They've now committed to a maximum of twenty patients a day and found ways to cut costs. In short, she became conscious of her worry, asked (and answered) the right questions, and set boundaries.

When working on your particular math problem, make balance part of the solution. I firmly believe in celebrating wins, taking breaks, and investing in life outside of the clinic. Even doctors need sustained personal growth outside of work.

In this spirit, Julia's decided to reevaluate her personal priorities too. She renews her gym membership, commits to a regular bedtime, cuts back on sweets, and finally starts planning that vacation with her spouse.

As a result, she begins to feel less stress and more command over her personal resources—until she gets a curveball, in the form of a certified letter, hand-delivered to her door.

NEXT STEPS

1. Notice when and why you tell yourself you're not enough.
2. When anxiety strikes, identify your unanswered questions—and answer them.

3. Note where you need boundaries and use all four steps to set, communicate, and reinforce those.

BOSS PODCAST EPISODES:

https://www.BOSSsurgery.com/podcasts/
boss-business-of-surgery-series

Ep. 30: *Decreasing Burnout and Stress, with Dr. Robyn Tiger the Stressfree MD*

Ep. 39: *Treat Yourself Like an Elite Athlete, with Dr. Getta Lal*

Ep. 51: *We Are All at Risk of Physician Suicide, with Dr. Michelle Chestovich*

Ep. 63: *Comparison Is the Thief of Joy (How RVUs Make Us Miserable)*

Ep. 46: *You Can Create Brave Boundaries, with Sasha Shillcut*

Ep. 33: *Boundaries Build Relationships*

CHAPTER 18

MALPRACTICE

Julia's home, finally resting, when she hears the doorbell. The postal worker has her sign before handing her the certified letter—from a law firm. She rips open the envelope to find a letter of intent to sue for malpractice related to a complication from a surgery she assisted with last year. While that patient made a full recovery, he nevertheless decided to sue.

Of course, she thinks. *Just as I commit to more work-life balance—a crisis!* Julia recently hired support at work, successfully argued for new equipment, and established herself as a senior partner—maybe even one poised to someday take over the practice as medical director—and now she's being sued.

The overwhelming dread reminds Julia of an earlier time, when a patient filed a state medical board complaint against her. While that complaint was ultimately resolved, it involved a big hassle—and plenty of self-pity.

After the initial shock of the lawsuit fades, a wave of resentment floods in: *I've been working so hard*, she thinks. *I don't deserve this. I wasn't even the lead surgeon on that operation. How could this happen to me?* Julia can't believe this threat—this *intrusion*—got to her front door.

Suddenly, even her home feels less safe, and fears cloud her thoughts: *What will my patients think? Will they find out? Will I lose everything?* Just when she'd hit her stride, this event retriggers her deficit mindset.

Julia already knows that, when applying for privileges at a hospital or practice, one of the intake questions is: "Have you ever been sued for malpractice?" To verify, employers can check a national practitioner database of malpractice lawsuits. *What if this impacts my employability?* she wonders.

As always, Julia has options. She can catastrophize the situation and spiral into irrational fear—exposure, financial ruin, professional exile—followed by shame, isolation, and overwhelm. Or she can educate herself on the facts.

Here's a great one to start with: More than half of all physicians will be named in a malpractice suit at some point in their careers. If you're a surgeon, that number rises to nearly 80 percent.

Medical board complaints are also more common than you think, especially since these don't require either a lawyer or a filing fee. In other words, every single one of us is more likely than not to face the stress of a medical board complaint or malpractice suit—and worrying about it does exactly nothing to help.

INSURANCE

While it may not *help* to worry, that certified letter tends to inspire panic in the best of us. All facts aside, it really can *feel* like you're about to lose everything you've worked so hard to achieve.

So here's a question: What if you could pay to not have this worry? What if you could simply write a check and relax, knowing your assets are now protected? And how much would you pay for that security? Would you pay five figures a year?

Guess what? You already do.

With few exceptions, all physicians carry malpractice insurance, although the limits and types of insurance vary. Indeed, most hospitals require proof of malpractice insurance to hold privileges to work in the hospital. As an employed physician, you may not think about it, since the cost of your malpractice insurance likely comes out of your pay behind the scenes. Meanwhile, for me and others who run a private practice, it's harder to ignore; I personally write the check every June.

Julia's lawsuit may have felt like it came out of nowhere, but it didn't. We have malpractice insurance (and legal counsel) for a reason—not to eliminate the risk of lawsuits, but to protect ourselves and our assets from their impact.

Lawyers know this too. I once saw a video ad by a local attorney who said something like, "I know you like your doctor, but that's what they have malpractice insurance for!"

What a shameless grab! I thought. *May as well go rob a bank!*

After all, it's FDIC insured. No harm done, right? A "victimless crime." Here's this lawyer apparently trying to convince patients to go after even those physicians who have worked hard to serve them well and build strong relationships because *no problem, right?*—malpractice insurance protects them from abject ruin. *Go ahead and cash in!*

Once I got past the impulse to punch the guy in the face, I realized he's actually right, in a way. That *is* why we have malpractice insurance. This painful annual five-figure fee is literally the price we pay to not have to worry. Even if we do get sued for malpractice, we've already taken the most important steps to protect ourselves.

Malpractice insurance contracts vary widely in terms of cost and coverage. Larger medical groups enjoy discounts, while independent locum tenens physicians tend to pay considerably more. I run a small private surgical practice, but we belong to a practice management group that qualifies us for a malpractice insurance discount.

As noted in Chapter 4, the statute of limitations for malpractice suits tends to be around two years, sometimes longer. When you start a new job, always negotiate tail coverage that protects you down the road should you leave.

If you did not negotiate that tail coverage in your last job, you haven't necessarily lost coverage. You can either negotiate nose insurance—which retroactively covers the same period of time—from your new employer, or you can cover it yourself. Just bear in mind that individual plans get costly.

Get to know your claims team at the malpractice insurance

company. You don't have to wait until you get sued to learn about the process—for example, whether they cover legal fees and what attorneys are in the insurance panel. If you have or know a lawyer you want to work with, see about getting them on your insurance company's panel in advance. That way, should a lawsuit come down, you'll have confidence in the person handling your claim.

PREVENTION

The lawyer in that predatorial ad tried to frame malpractice suits as some victimless transaction, but when you're personally affected by a suit, it doesn't feel victimless. It feels like a threat to everything you hold dear—and it can cause very real emotional damage.

But as BOSS MDs, we know victims are powerless. So let's rewrite this story. How do we prevent malpractice suits and take our power back? Where is our power in the first place? Put it another way: What in this situation falls within our control?

One aspect we control is how we operate professionally. We can do our best work for our patients—to care for them, build a rapport, and earn their trust. Aside from malpractice insurance, solid patient relationships are your number one prevention against lawsuits.

As we covered in Chapter 9 (on complications), patients want us to assure them on three main points:

1. That we're there for them.
2. That we care about them.

3. That we have a solution for their problem and can communicate it clearly.

Beyond that, they just want to know what happened to them and what's going to happen next.

Patients are far more likely to file a malpractice suit following a bad experience with a physician who does not communicate well and/or seem to care. These patients may not fully understand what's happened, and they've lost trust in their doctor or medical team. They turn to this third party legal firm, who claims to protect their interests, while often pushing underinformed, self-interested interpretations of what might have happened and why.

You're likely already taking the most important steps to prevent both complications and malpractice suits—by making every patient a partner in their own care. This means fully informing and reminding them about risks, empowering them to make their own decisions, and communicating every step of the way about options, expectations, and potential outcomes.

If and when you face negative outcomes, address the problem immediately and thoroughly, reminding the patient of your previous discussions, their documented role in the decision making, and their (signed) informed consent.

Of course, we can do our best, document everything, build strong patient relationships, and still get sued. Just as we cannot eliminate all risk of medical complications, we cannot escape litigation risk.

SUPPORT

It's easy to panic about lawsuits because no one talks about them—in part because they're stressful and embarrassing, but also because we're not allowed to.

Isolation compounds shame and fear. But while reaching out to trusted sources and communicating about problems helps us cultivate shame resilience, typically a gag order restricts physicians from openly discussing malpractice suits.

That doesn't mean there's no support. If you get a letter of intent to sue, start by talking kindly to yourself. Rather than catastrophizing the situation, remind yourself that this happens to most doctors and you've already invested in malpractice insurance to protect yourself.

You're not alone. Call your malpractice carrier, talk to the risk management team at work, and hire an attorney. While you may not be able to discuss details of the case with your partner, family, or friends, you should still reach out to loved ones for general support. It also helps to speak to a professional therapist who's bound by law to hold all information in strict confidentiality.

Sometimes our reactions to situations cause more psychological damage than the situations themselves. Mental health practitioners can help us examine how we respond to and process perceived threats.

Finally, ask your attorney to help you understand the legal process. If you've never gone through something like this before, it all feels very personal. Every motion, every spat between lawyers—can all hit like a series of gut punches. But understanding the legal process in advance helps you realize that most of this really isn't about you.

The plaintiff may sue various parties or file extra motions for purely strategic reasons. They understand that most parties will get dropped and motions dismissed. Sit down with your counsel to review the case in detail. If your attorney can't or won't explain things to you, ask to meet with their paralegal or a claims adjuster (or get a new lawyer).

PERSPECTIVE

Getting sued is scary. We worry that we're going to lose money, or even our medical license. We think our colleagues and patients will find out and abandon us.

But that letter can't hurt us. What hurts us are these stories we're spinning, along with the worry, resentment, and fear. Don't make yourself a victim before anything's happened. Observe the negative emotions without buying into them wholesale and letting them carry you away.

The letter's just a problem to solve. Besides, if you've been paying your malpractice insurance and you've built good relationships with your patients, you've likely already solved the problem. Often, your malpractice policy has a rider for legal defense related to medical board complaints as well, in which case, you're covered there too.

What's more, just because you've been served a letter, it doesn't mean you'll actually be sued. Similarly, just because someone files a complaint, it doesn't mean the board will agree or take punitive action. Most malpractice lawyers encourage their clients to name every single doctor who touched either the patient or their chart, including someone who just covered for the weekend, or who rounded once and wrote a note. Lawyers tend to cast as wide a net as possible then drop names along the way

Because the majority of doctors get named in a malpractice suit at some point, the best you can do is pay for malpractice insurance and build strong patient relationships. If and when that letter comes, rely on professional support—your malpractice carrier, risk management professionals at work, legal counsel, and therapist—to minimize the collateral damage caused by shame, fear, and isolation.

Don't forget about tactical empathy. We need to accept human fallibility, both in ourselves and in others. One way to neutralize the victim-villain narrative is to accept the humanity of everyone involved.

Granted, you may feel natural resentment towards the person who sues and/or their lawyer, but that's not productive. If we, as physicians, want to be accepted for making mistakes, we should also accept that other humans are dealing with their own problems. For whatever reason, suing felt like the choice they needed to make. Maybe they're trying to scam you, but probably they're just trying to protect or stand up for themselves.

Whatever led them to take this action, we can't know their innermost thoughts and feelings, and we don't have to. We can still choose how we react to their actions. We can protect and stand up for ourselves.

RESOLUTION

Julia's letter of intent to sue doesn't bode the end of the world, nor even of her career. After discussing the matter with her attorney, her insurance carrier, and her colleagues at work, Julia realizes just how common—and manageable—this kind of thing is.

To help manage stress, Julia makes an appointment with a trusted mental health professional, who helps her process her feelings, examine her self-talk, and identify practical coping skills. Several months later, Julia learns she's been dropped from the case.

She came out of this experience having reconnected with her therapist and learned invaluable lessons. Moving forward, she accepts the risk of litigation as a fact, and she knows how to prepare for this possibility and find support.

Experiencing this financial and professional uncertainty—and coming out the other side unscathed—actually helps Julia feel more resilient and confident. She realizes how much she's learned about herself and her work relationships. She's empowered herself to improve outcomes, educate herself about clinical finances, and emerge as a leader at her practice. All her hard work has freed up time and bandwidth to grow professionally. In the next chapter, we'll talk about how to likewise cultivate more abundance in your *personal* life.

NEXT STEPS

1. Get to know points of contact at your malpractice insurance carrier and among your risk management team.

2. Proactively seek support when concerned about a patient interaction.
3. Prevent litigation by building solid patient relationships through transparent, supportive communications.

BOSS PODCAST EPISODES:

https://www.BOSSsurgery.com/podcasts/
boss-business-of-surgery-series

Ep. 4: *The MedMal Coach Talks about Litigation Stress*

CHAPTER 19

FROM THRIFT TO WEALTH

Julia was trained to grind. Residency taught her to hustle and strive—to *go, go, go*. Lately though, she's beginning to question that approach—especially since she and her husband, Rob, took the plunge and started growing their own family. Since welcoming their daughter, Sophie, Julia's adapted to caring for an infant while healing from childbirth, followed by day care costs, sick days, and the increasing desire to spend more time at home with family.

She's been managing it all, but with a nagging suspicion that she can't keep it up much longer. Julia begins to wonder, *Is the goal of this one human life really to make $400,000 a year by utterly burning myself out?*

To launch a career in medicine, we work hard to build knowledge and skills, often while depriving ourselves of sleep, leisure time, and material indulgences. If you apply the BOSS MD lessons in this book, you can build back, not only seeing gains in your bank account, but also in your available energy, time, and expertise, as well as job flexibility.

You can proactively avoid burnout and empower yourself to better manage your assets. This requires deprogramming the deficit mindset and shifting to a mentality of abundance. In other words, switch the dial from thrift to wealth.

When we hear "wealth," most of us think of money. And yes, you should experience financial gains to compensate for your work, pay educational debt, and build a comfortable, meaningful life.

But this chapter focuses on more than that. When it comes to developing an abundance mindset, time and energy matters as much as—if not more than—financial gains. I'd argue that these are our most precious and limited resources.

ABUNDANCE MINDSET

Especially when we start out weighed down by academic debt, we tend to push ourselves to always work harder and earn more. It's possible to go too far, depriving ourselves of time, rest, and variety. Because we're not machines, this leads to burnout and resentment. We find ourselves envious of people with more relaxed lifestyles. We delay or deny ourselves vacations—or hesitate to build a family out of fear that we won't be able to sustain it all.

I no longer allow my career to control me. Instead, I've taken command of my time and my choices. As I do, I'm becoming more interested in how to enhance my health, invest in hobbies and interests, and better use my time than I am in increasing the numbers in my bank account.

The deficit mindset is fixed. It claims there's a set amount of earning potential and only one way to get everything done. The alternative—the abundance mindset—questions this assumption. It says things like "work smarter, not harder." It values time and quality of life as much as financial wealth.

In residency, we focus on fixed goal posts within a set system. We know the structure we're working within. As we move up the ranks, we often work even harder and longer hours.

It took me a long time to untether from the grind. I took a chance by leaving a secure position as an employed surgeon, and I worked extremely hard to get a private practice up and running.

Then, I reevaluated my priorities and looked for ways to increase time and energy, while maintaining a healthy bottom line. Hiring PAs and NPs to help at my practice widens our funnel, allowing us to serve more patients and earn more. I didn't realize how much time it also had freed up for me until I co-signed fifty notes in one week—fifty notes I didn't have to write. This helped me realize that, if I continued to dial things in, I could revolutionize the way that I approach my work.

GROWTH DAYS

This allowed me to make a radical—previously unthinkable—change in my life: I began taking every Wednesday off. I call them "growth days." Rather than directly supervising the flow of patients and clinical work, I instead use this time to grow.

Any given Wednesday, I decide what "growth" looks like. Some weeks, that means leaning into my CEO duties, figuring out how to better manage my business and plan strategies for working smarter. Other weeks, that means catching up on podcast editing, writing, or some other professional side quest.

At first, this was very disconcerting. In fact, I felt like a bum. I had no idea how to support myself, so it felt selfish. I initially rebelled by sabotaging my own growth time. But eventually, I realized I was doing something constructive and even necessary. I regained control over my schedule, began looking at things in new ways, and discovered solutions I might not have otherwise seen.

Give most surgeons a "growth day," and watch them quickly fill it with more work related to their clinical day-to-day. Because that's all we know. Given "free time," most of us feel restless or guilty. We may even show up to clinic anyway and start seeing patients. That's because we still associate our time and effort with *money*.

Money is not the only way to measure value. If you can diligently protect non-clinical growth time, you'll gain new perspectives, learn new patterns, and even find new ways to become more efficient.

I recently spent part of a Wednesday afternoon creating educational handouts for patients. While this doesn't result in an immediate exchange of time for money, the investment has saved me hours of counseling time and built trust with my patients, improving outcomes and streamlining clinical encounters.

This represents a complete mind shift of who we are as professionals, because it allows us to move from the worker-bee hourly grind to the CEO, the visionary and leader—the ultimate BOSS MD.

DITCH THE NUMBERS GAME

On one of my social media networks, someone recently posted: "All I have to do is suffer six more years at this job that I hate." My mental response was: *Who the hell came up with that number?*

So often, we feel trapped in a cage we put ourselves in, beholden to timelines we've invented ourselves. A lot of this comes from paying back educational debt within a deficit mindset: "I have to do X for Y years, working at Z job until I can pay back my loans and finally be happy."

It's easy to fall into the numbers game, especially when you've been trained to chase goalposts and metrics. You've internalized the idea that you're responsible for everything, and there's one conventional, formulaic way to achieve.

Often, the cost is physician burnout. Instead, recalculate how much you actually need to live and be happy. As the CEO of my own practice, I hire front desk staff for less than $20 an hour, and they somehow survive. So the fear that unless I exhaust myself as a physician I'll lose everything and perish is somewhat silly.

We often compare ourselves to what we think our colleagues might be making, or to what we think we should be making. But those are arbitrary numbers perpetuating our hustle-culture anxiety. Reframe the math problem by asking yourself, *How much do I need to live?*

Then answer the question for yourself. Chances are, you don't need to stress yourself out as much as you think.

How do we ditch the numbers game? First, recognize that we made it all up. Sure, you could commit to six years of misery at a job you can't stand. Or you could consider finding a job you don't hate, changing your loan payment goal, or finding ways to downsize.

In Chapter 1, we talked about how envy can help reveal your true desires and values. Pay attention to the patterns and lifestyles of the people you secretly resent. Often, successful people in high-powered careers find themselves annoyed by those who earn much less but are able to reduce work hours and take time off for family.

If you hate your job, you're not showing up as your best self, so your growth curve suffers. Why spend six years essentially devaluing yourself and your time in a job you're not innately invested in? While you may achieve some financial goals, everything else in your life loses value.

STOP PLAYING SMALL

The deficit mindset keeps us in jobs that don't work for us. It tells us this is the best we can do. It ties us to what we believe we're capable of right now. Therefore, we're not living up to or even imagining what we have the potential to become. We're too busy grinding away at keeping the job we're good at now to evolve into the BOSS MDs we're meant to be.

In short, by stretching ourselves thin, we're playing small.

Growing into your potential could mean running your own private practice, or switching to locum tenens and traveling the world. As physicians, it's easy to feel trapped by the limitations of an hourly rate, but when you begin to truly value your time and energy, you find you can do much more.

It goes back to knowing yourself and understanding where you thrive. What thoughts and emotions do you have about your current job? What thoughts and emotions do you have when doing a side gig or thinking about other possibilities? Where are you playing small or selling yourself short?

Maybe your side gig adjunct teaching at a university is what you really love, but you maintain primary employment at a large, for-profit medical system because it feels more secure. Maybe you fantasize about leaving clinical work altogether and instead consulting or coaching—but after investing so much, you feel like you owe it to yourself or your colleagues to grind on.

No one knows the answer for you. What works for me may not work for you. That's why I'm in the business of coaching people to define what BOSS MD means for them, not to prescribe a specific lifestyle formula.

Beware of advice based on the thoughts and experiences (and sometimes insecurities) of other people. They're often playing small too, and secretly resentful of those who think (or climb) outside of the box. "I had to suffer through this, so you should too" tends to be the underlying message, as well as: "This is just the way it's done."

As individuals, we do face some limitations, in terms of time, energy, and effort. All the more reason to avoid giving away all our energy to jobs and systems that drain our energy and exploit our efforts. This includes energy wasted complaining about huge, overwhelming problems in our field.

Focus on innovating solutions to those things within your control. This frees up energy to examine what is and isn't working, and how you can create a life that better supports, challenges, and nurtures you.

This lesson hearkens back to Chapter 8 (Advocacy), in a way that seems paradoxical. Sometimes, what keeps us playing small is worrying too much about some scary big picture that's none of our business. When we disengage from that bigger picture and instead focus on our own personal values and desires, our lives—and our impact—can truly grow and expand.

CLEAN UP YOUR SIDE OF THE STREET

By doing what inspires and nurtures you, you show up for yourself and others differently. When you clean up your side of the street, neighbors are more likely to see that and respond in kind. Either way, at least your side of the street is better now, and that's where you are.

We regularly underestimate the impact of individual choices

and habits in part because we're discouraged by the bigger picture. If you think too much about the full magnitude of global disasters, why even recycle? It's not going to make much of a difference. But just as these small choices add up to big change, our daily habits influence others and build new individual and collective ways to live and work.

The advocacy chapter subverts expectations a bit by focusing more on individual behaviors than on lobbying or marching for a cause. Similarly, when we allow ourselves white space on our calendar to brainstorm a new approach, or we take the time to adequately train and delegate support staff, these small investments pay dividends.

When we work ourselves to the bone, then scrimp and save to save every single penny and sacrifice every waking minute, we're not fully engaged with or invested in our lives. We're not mindfully connecting with our patients. Instead, we're spreading anxiety and perpetuating the hustle culture we've trained under: *If I work harder, I'll succeed.*

Not only is that approach not nourishing to our souls or sustainable, it's also not scalable. To excel cannot mean endlessly pouring time and effort into what we're already doing, because these resources are limited. If you slow down long enough to see things differently, you can adjust operations and find pockets of time. Such small investments can create exponential growth—as well as professional freedom and flexibility.

Julia's career began as a hustle. Slowly, she began to optimize her life, proactively managing her mindset, habits, and resources. Her practice has become more efficient over time, and her quality of life has improved—even as both her family and her responsibilities grow.

As she adapts to a new work-life balance, she realizes she also has more options. She's built the skills to open a solo practice, or she can stay and continue moving up the ranks.

Lately though, her thoughts keep returning to her daughter, Sophie. Julia wonders if she *should* continue expanding her career. Maybe she'd rather figure out how to dial it back and invest more time at home—even have another child?

Ultimately, there are no "right or wrong" answers. The next and final chapter will discuss how to navigate, and best direct, career (and life) shifts as a medical doctor.

NEXT STEPS

1. Evaluate how you *truly* define success (versus. how you think you're "supposed to").
2. Review any metrics you currently use to measure success. Do these align with your definition of success? If not, make new ones.
3. Carve out space for growth time within your schedule. Expand this over time.

BOSS PODCAST EPISODES:

https://www.BOSSsurgery.com/podcasts/
boss-business-of-surgery-series

Ep. 1: *Growth Days*

Ep. 60: *When a Big System Doesn't Understand What You Do, with Dr. Steve Siegal*

Ep. 54: *Opening a Surgery Center, with Dr. Seaworth*

Ep. 57: *Creating the Culture You Want with Private Practice, with Dr. Melanie Seybt*

CHAPTER 20

CAREER SHIFTS

Julia's come far from her early days, hustling within a system she didn't well understand. With each step along the way, she faced a steep learning curve—and that's perfectly normal. As we enter new phases of life, we naturally apply old lenses and mindsets to the new thing before expanding ourselves. It may feel clumsy at first, but with struggle comes adaptation and growth.

It's important to not get too comfortable with one job, role, or way of doing things. Even if we aren't actively seeking change, it comes to us, especially when we pick a job that doesn't align with our values, or outgrow our current roles, or a family event causes us to move house or reduce hours.

This final chapter is all about learning to embrace, and even drive, the plot twist. It discusses how to proactively drive those changes to suit you, rather than constantly reacting to changes and mindlessly sacrificing your time, energy, and well-being out of fear.

Julia's reached a point in her career where she can pursue a leadership role or even launch her own practice. Or she can scale back her career to focus more on family building. Or both! Regardless, if she makes the decision based on her own values and goals rather than what she thinks she's "supposed to do," it's a boss move.

We've talked about creating boundaries around time and other resources. Navigating career shifts follows that same concept. When you become purposeful about setting goals, priorities, and boundaries, you'll find those thresholds change over time. Maybe you want to grow into a leadership role, or maybe you'd rather pursue more flexibility to free up time for non-clinical passions.

This is your story. You can choose different cases. You can leave the for-profit world to teach medical students and conduct research. You can even set up streams of passive income and phase out of clinical life completely.

EXPAND YOUR IDENTITY

If you over-identify with one way to work, any shift feels like a threat to your identity. You may start thinking, *That's not for me, because* this *is who I am.*

Ultimately though, you're not your job. This means you can choose what to do. It also means that your off-time is not just for figuring out how to exponentially grow your practice, but also for investing in yourself so that when you're retired, you know what to do with yourself.

One of the biggest recent trends is toward more flexibility in practice. Increasingly, physicians are choosing locum tenens work or reducing hours to better respond to life's curveballs, like having kids or caring for an aging parent.

Nature doesn't model constant linear growth, but instead cycles of activity and abundance, followed by periods of relative rest and austerity. Animals go along with it, but we humans often panic when we need to rest and recover, or switch jobs, or address a financial loss. For some reason we've tied our sense of who we are and what we're worth to this impossible ideal of constant, predictable gains—every quarter of every year in every industry.

You've gotten where you are because of hard work. While hard work never goes out of style, the trick now is to evolve. You can do your work in an easier, more efficient way. You can get other people to help you. Once you free up more time and effort, you may find your mentality beginning to shift.

The life of a medical doctor can be more than decades of employed hustle, followed by a hard stop. Instead of over-identifying with what you're capable of right now, you can learn to live toward your potential. By expanding your self-worth to include more than your job title and salary, you become more responsive to unforeseen events in your life, and learn to trust the process.

ASK SIMPLE QUESTIONS

We're told to stay in our lanes. To work hard within one field, or even within one organization or role, until we retire or die. But the truth is that most of us advance to new positions or switch jobs altogether. And many choose to cut back hours or take breaks to address a personal matter at some point.

No one trains us to ask the simple questions: *How many cases do you really need to support your career as a surgeon? How many hours do you need to work? Is the pay cut of working for a teaching university worth the value of teaching and mentoring?*

Contrary to what others—or your own mind—may be telling you, there is no set answer, no set number. No one formula for success. Plus, the pace and flow of work will naturally change throughout your employment and well into retirement.

Rather than hustling miserably for some future payoff in retirement, ask yourself: *How can I expand my identity, now and always? How can I direct how my career progresses, proactively planning for future phases and evolving into them?*

EMBRACE THE POSSIBILITY OF FAILURE

Once you become comfortable with one way of doing things, it feels harder to do something different. It's comforting to cling to the status quo. After all, what if you fail?

When I walked out of a secure but dissatisfying hospital job, I took a risk. I had no backup plan. My contract limited my local employment, and I'd never been an entrepreneur before. What did I know about starting my own surgical private practice?

The answer is, not much—at first. But I learned. I challenged my notion of who I was and what I could do, and it stretched. Now I have a thriving, profitable practice that affords me enough time to pursue other professional projects and enjoy time with family. I'm also a landlord, a podcast host, and a coach for physicians, providing opportunities for other people to reclaim their power and become their version of the BOSS MD.

All because I was willing to accept the possibility of failure.

In Chapter 1, we talked about how your personality is more verb than noun. The same applies to your career path. It doesn't need to follow some prescribed linear path. Nor does it need to stagnate and settle.

Normalize career transitions from the beginning to the end. Even perceived failures—the false starts, incompatible job fits, or failed business ideas—help you evolve. Our own doubts and self-imposed limitations hurt us far more than trying and failing.

When self-doubt shows up, address it head on. When it asks, *How do I know I can do this?*, simply look back at all you've done. Notice how, every time you take on something new, you stretch and grow.

Author E.L. Doctorow once likened writing a novel to driving through fog at night. "You can only see as far as your headlights, but you can make the whole trip that way." The same applies to all life choices. You don't need to see five miles down the road; you can't respond to it yet. You can only respond to what's right in front of you. The rest will come into view when it's supposed to.

Next time you're looking for a job, realize that five or ten years ago, you had no idea you'd be where you are right now. You didn't need to know. Practice gratitude for all you've experienced, achieved, and learned so far, and give yourself the trust and confidence you've earned.

PROTECT YOURSELF

Sometimes, career shifts aren't your choice. Something may happen to you that prevents you from engaging with the career you worked so hard to build. That's why it's so important to invest in good disability insurance.

Disability insurance covers a portion of your gross pre-tax income if you cannot work due to debilitating illness, injury, or cognitive challenges. You choose how long after the triggered event checks will arrive (often thirty to ninety days or more), and you receive tax-free income like a paycheck.

Much like the legalities of contract negotiation, disability insurance is an important and complex topic—so you'll want to seek help from an expert (and that's not me).

Life insurance is another important consideration. It protects your loved ones from any debt you may have incurred and from the impact of lost income. Whole life insurance remains in place for as long as you pay premiums and term life insurance is based on the number of years you choose. Again, do your research and talk to a professional.

LIVE YOUR LEGACY

My personal journey took me from a life of hustle and achievement to one of service. That's where I find satisfaction in life, not from growing my bank account or outpacing everyone around me, but through serving.

When most people think of legacy, they think estate planning. But legacy is much more than how the story ends. It's the entire journey, plot twist by plot twist. It's not about how a life ends, but how it's lived along the way.

For me, service mainly has to do with the patients I treat and support, but also my influence on colleagues, clients, and anyone who takes the time to listen to my podcast or read this book. It's how I raise my children and treat my family and friends. It's recognizing the ripples I put out, the impact I leave on the world.

When we only chase personal achievement, we reduce our story to accolades and earnings—which feel hollow after a while. We spend all our time and energy outsourcing validation or fulfilling someone else's version of ourselves, and ultimately (sorry to say) no one cares. In the end, people rarely remember your awards, or how much money you earned. But they do remember the impact you had on their lives—how you made them feel. Your service will be far more impactful when you show up in an authentic way.

Maybe Julia continues to take on more influence at work. Maybe she decides to leave and start her own practice. Or maybe she decides to take extended unpaid leave to have another child. While she can't predict every outcome or ensure a fixed notion of "success," Julia can become the hero of her own story by actively living the legacy she wants to leave.

We don't always pick how the story starts, but we can determine the ending based on how we respond. Own your story. Expand it. Embrace the plot shifts that reveal themselves one chapter at a time. When it comes to major shifts in your career and life, recognize that you will grow into them.

NEXT STEPS

1. Plan for both voluntary and involuntary changes in your career.
2. Speak with a life and disability insurance expert to ensure the right coverage for each stage of life.

BOSS PODCAST EPISODES:

https://www.BOSSsurgery.com/podcasts/
boss-business-of-surgery-series

Ep. 29: *When You Love Your Career, but Life Happens, with Dr. Riikka Mohorn*

Ep. 38: *Creating a Schedule That Works and Taking a Year Off, with Dr. Beth Johnston*

Ep. 26: *Permission to Have the Life You Want, with Dr. Sharon McLaughlin, Founder of Female Physician Entrepreneurs Group and Mindlull.com*

Ep. 16: *Finding the Joy in Surgery Again by Abandoning the Path, with Dr. Serene Shereef*

Ep. 52: *Protecting Yourself with Disability Insurance, with Dr. Stephanie Pearson*

Ep. 13: *Doing What You Love Is Not Selfish, with Dr. Janelle Wagner*

Ep. 9: *Transitioning Out of Surgery, Self-Care, and Boundaries, with Dr. Victoria Silas*

CONCLUSION

Julia started out within a huge, for-profit medical system where she felt like a tiny cog in a machine. After moving to private practice, she struggled to find her voice, navigate interpersonal dynamics, and grow her patient base within the practice's eat-what-you-kill model. Eventually though, she established herself as a business-savvy senior partner.

Along the way, she made mistakes and fell into unhelpful patterns. From surgical complications to administrative overwhelm to malpractice panic, Julia at times questioned her worth as a physician. However, it's because of—not in spite of—these challenges that she kept growing, expanding, and becoming her personal version of the BOSS MD.

The same goes for all of us. I can't think of a single compelling tale in which the protagonist never makes a mistake or faces a problem. There's always resistance, tension, obstacles along the way. That's what makes a good story.

Not to say Julia's character arc would make a hit TV series. For that level of storytelling, we'd need some serious stakes: crime, sex, tragedy, danger—the works. For the purposes of this book, I aimed to make Julia's post-residency medical career path relevant and relatable. You don't need cinematic levels of drama to forge a hero's journey.

Let's face it, physician burnout isn't exactly sensational. It mostly concerns day-to-day stressors, processes, and pitfalls. The frustration—and exhaustion—builds slowly as we struggle to promote our practice, manage work relationships, or navigate the endless streams of insurance claims and clinical notes.

This book poses one small but vital question: *What if you're not stuck at all?*

RECLAIM THE STORY

In our simultaneously tedious and high-pressure careers, how do we reclaim power and grow into well-rounded abundance? If you're beginning to apply the BOSS MD strategies outlined in this book, you're well on your way.

You're beginning to examine stories you tell yourself—your beliefs and assumptions—both about yourself and about those around you. This allows you to identify your values and goals, lead with your strengths, and reframe problems as potential. It also helps you define your unique version of success, then discern and negotiate the best professional fit as you **establish your career.**

To **find your voice**, you're unpacking resistance to self-promotion and tapping patients as your best marketing assets. You're navigating difficult relationships and group dynamics through visualization techniques, self-validation, and better listening. All of this helps you advocate for yourself and issues you care about, either through public activism or simply how you show up in the world everyday.

By tracking your performance and collaboratively delegating, you're finding ways to **improve outcomes**. Now you can identify—and side-step—perfection traps, from streamlining clinical notes to cultivating shame resilience when things go wrong.

You've also begun to **follow the money** by learning about coding, reimbursement, insurance, and clinical finances. Once you shift to a mindset of empowerment and curiosity, you'll better understand industry mechanics, gain budgetary insight, and grow into someone who's earned a prominent place at the table—a valuable partner and leader.

Finally, you're applying that same curiosity and business savvy to **protect your assets,** shifting from a deficit mindset to one that values time, energy, and lifestyle as much as material wealth—all while embracing plot twists, covering your ass(ets) with malpractice—as well as disability and life—insurance, honoring your boundaries, and living your legacy. These practices help you switch the dial from thrift to wealth, growing your career and expanding your life.

When we stretch ourselves thin, we end up playing small. But we can address and prevent burnout by reclaiming our personal stories. In the story of your life, would you rather play the role of an endlessly suffering victim, or of the hero who faces obstacles and overcomes them?

We reclaim our stories by actively choosing a mindset that empowers us to take back time, energy, and agency. First, by dropping the pointless resistance and resentment currently eroding our bandwidth. Then, by establishing and enforcing boundaries that protect the time and energy we're building back into our lives. Finally, by consistently showing up with courage, curiosity, and compassion—for ourselves and others—we help ensure that each action and interaction yields a more constructive and fruitful effect.

BOSS MD MENTALITY

Many physicians tell themselves a story of overwhelm. They feel overworked, disrespected, and trapped in an impersonal and deeply flawed medical system. Each time some new frustration arises—say, a sudden schedule change—it whips up all those rehearsed and interconnected tales of injustice and outrage. It's so easy to ruminate on everything that's wrong with the system, to get worked up into an inner frenzy, followed by a *maybe-I'm-not-cut-out-for-this* crash bordering on despair.

Becoming the BOSS MD requires a complete mind shift: From the worker-bee hourly grind to the CEO, the visionary and leader. It challenges us to take full responsibility, not only for our outcomes, but also for our beliefs, emotions, and boundaries. It's a deep dive process—and one that never stops—but in the end, we learn to thrive within and help improve a system made up not just of codes, claims, and contracts—but of real people, just like us.

You don't have to become the chief medical officer at some large hospital or CEO of your own practice. Your hero's journey could look like switching to part-time employment while you grow your family, or becoming an independent contractor as a locum tenens. Whether you make a career move or stay where you are, you can become the BOSS MD by understanding and honoring yourself, embracing the plot twists—and knowing when to initiate twists of your own.

Change is the point. Our careers are verbs, not nouns—and the same goes for us. When I first started out as a surgeon, I tried to fit the mold of a hard ass authoritative surgeon. Now I apply my true strengths as a supportive, empathetic coach and leader.

Similarly, it's time to shed the unintentional, unexamined identity somebody else gave you, and instead discover who you really are and what you're truly capable of. Not by proving yourself to others, but by consciously choosing where you develop your power and how you serve others.

"Doctor" is an identity you've already earned—and you get to decide what to do with that. Walt Whitman once said, "I contain multitudes," and he was right. We all do, even if we tell ourselves otherwise.

In the end, people rarely remember your awards or how much money you earned. But they do remember the impact you had on their lives. And your service will be far more impactful when you show up in an authentic way.

Once I got honest about who I am, what I want, and what I can do—my whole life transformed. I evolved from a nervous young attending who thought she had to shout to have a voice to a confident senior surgeon who directs her own practice and empowers fellow physicians.

Many tips I share in this book seem small. Learning about coding, clinical note taking, collaborative delegation—it's not exactly the stuff of revolution. But even small changes in how we operate can have an exponential impact, both on our lives and on the industry and world around us.

This book is part of my exponential impact. Now it's your turn.

You're not someone's resident or intern anymore. You are a badass BOSS MD attending. And now, you get to choose: You can outsource your power to external forces—or you can dig deeper, regain your personal and professional autonomy, and reconnect with what you love about medicine.

The rest of the story is up to you.

ACKNOWLEDGMENTS

To my parents, Emory and Cheryl Deason, and my sister, Lori Jordan: Thank you for supporting my overachieving efforts, giving me room to make mistakes, and encouraging me to follow my own path.

To William: There aren't enough words. If everyone had a William, we would change the world. You hold space for me to relax, get creative, and accept adventure. You always support the "me" projects—which so often become "we" projects. Thank you for all you do for me and Charlotte and Sophie; they are better people with you as their father.

To my girls: I see the future in you, and I can't wait to see what you'll accomplish in this world.

To my BOSS MDs: You are a constant inspiration. From Gillian, the first person who hired me, to all my *BOSS* podcast listeners and every fellow surgeon who's given me the honor of being your coach—each one of you has made me better. We are the change. What we do matters.

To COL Shriver, my program director and fierce supporter: You believed in me when I didn't believe in myself, and your unwavering confidence made me better.

To Dr. A.J. Copeland, Dr. Mary Maniscalco-Theberge: You prove that leadership and inclusion happens at every level. Show up, do the work, insist on being heard, and lift others as you climb.

To Anita Martin: You are the antidote to my avoidant behavior. I didn't realize how challenging getting out of my own way could be; I appreciate all you've done to help.